365

Fascinating

FACTS

from the

WORLD OF

DISCOVERY

365

Fascinating

FACTS

from the

WORLD OF

DISCOVERY

Donald DeYoung

New Leaf Press

ISBN: 0-89221-500-3
Library of Congress Number: 00-102662

All Scripture is from the New International Version of the Bible unless otherwise noted.

Cover design by Farewell Communications

Printed in the United States of America.

Please visit our website for other great titles:
www.newleafpress.net

For information regarding publicity for author interviews contact Dianna Fletcher at (870) 438-5288.

INTRODUCTION

The pace of modern life accelerates with each new year. Too often the events of the past are remembered only dimly, if not forgotten entirely. And yet there is abundant wisdom to be found in historical details. This book attempts to engage one fascinating dimension of history, the role of *creation* in science and society. By creation I mean the biblical view of origins and human history. It was a steadfast belief in the Creator of the universe which helped shape America and also motivated many science discoveries worldwide. In the not-so-distant past there was a common belief that nature was intelligently planned and consistent, and it was therefore worthy of scientific study. One goal of this calendar is to remind us that many important landmarks regarding creation studies really did occur — some recently and others long ago. There is a rich heritage of creation awareness, worldwide. May this calendar encourage its study and appreciation. The book also serves as an almanac and a fact-finder.

No calendar of historical dates can be comprehensive. For each day of the year there are multiple possibilities for creation comments. I have therefore selected events of general interest. Some days have more than one item placed in the calendar. Birthdates of creationist and evolutionary personalities are generally avoided because they are cataloged elsewhere. Only those who have attempted to construct a historical calendar can fully appreciate the challenge undertaken. The chronology researcher's lament: There is nothing so difficult to discover as the unchangeable date! I have attempted to crosscheck and verify each of the entries. Major resources used are listed as references at the end of the book.

Historical dates are complicated by past variations of the calendar. The Gregorian calendar used today was adopted in 1582 by most Roman Catholic countries (see October 13). Other nations, however, slowly and only reluctantly adopted this revised calendar over the next three centuries. The American colonies waited until 1752. Thus, George Washington's birthday was February 11, 1732 in the old style calendar, then later changed to February 22 in the new style calendar. I have listed the traditionally recognized dates for all events, whether old or new style. Any calendar corrections, additions, or comments from readers would be appreciated by the author.

1801. The first and largest known asteroid was discovered today during studies of the heavens. Italian astronomer Giuseppe Piazzi (1746–1826) first located this asteroid, now called Ceres. It is named after the Roman goddess of the harvest, thus also our word "cereal."

Thousands of these large "rocks," some tens or hundreds of miles in size, circle the sun between the orbits of the planets Mars and Jupiter. Most are located more than 200 million miles outward from earth. An original small planet may have been pulverized by a collision, or perhaps the asteroid belt has been present since the creation week.

Asteroids are part of the endless variety that the Creator has placed within the solar system and the heavens beyond. In recent years there have been dire predictions of asteroid collisions with the earth, perhaps annihilating mankind. However, the earth's future is in God's hands.

• • • •

1925. The known universe suddenly grew much larger today when new findings were presented at a January conference. Astronomer Edwin Hubble (1889–1953) had determined that certain fuzzy objects in the night sky were faraway galaxies instead of nearby whirlpools of gas. These distant galaxies, each holding about 100 billion stars, are spread across space like countless remote islands. The universe is currently thought to be billions of light years in size. A single light year is nearly six trillion miles in length.

Genesis 1:16 declares that all the stars and galaxies were supernaturally formed on the fourth day of creation, by God's word.

JANUARY 2

1811. Today French chemist Benjamin Delessert succeeded in extracting crystalized sugar from beets. This was a major breakthrough in food production worldwide. Napoleon, emperor of France at this time, immediately devoted 600,000 acres of land to sugar beet cultivation. He also ordered the building of 40 processing factories. Sugar beets today are second only to sugarcane as the major source of the world's sugar supply.

Unlike tropical sugarcane, sugar beets can be grown in colder climates. Genetic research has gradually increased the sugar content of beets from 4 percent sugar to 17 percent. At this point a barrier has been reached, showing the limits of genetic change.

Agricultural experts continue to probe the great potential for food production that is built into nature. Food production has easily kept pace with the growing population over the centuries. Unfortunately, distribution problems, political instability, and greed often lead to food shortages in spite of the God-given abundance.

••••

1936. The electron vacuum tube was first described at a conference today. This device marked a major advance in electrical components. Amplifier tubes made radio reception possible. Also, particular types of vacuum tube are sensitive to ultraviolet and infrared light waves. They therefore can "see" in the dark. Such devices permit, for example, study of the activities of nocturnal or night-active creatures.

Our visible "window" of light for exploring the creation has been greatly expanded by modern electronics.

1989. The Human Genome Project was officially launched today in the United States. This is a group effort by thousands of biologists to map all the genes of the human body. Construction of this road map for our chromosomes required over a decade of genetic research.

The result is a better understanding of disease, heredity, and our created complexity. As with all research, the results have the potential of being used for either good or evil.

• • • •

Around this date the earth is positioned closest to the sun in its annual orbit. During January we are about four million miles closer to the sun than in July. This distance variation has little effect on the world's weather. Instead, the earth's seasons are controlled by the tilt of the earth's axis.

The Northern Hemisphere is tilted toward the sun during its summer season, and away from the sun during winter. January brings winter to the Northern Hemisphere and summer to the south. In January the earth is also moving fastest in its elliptical orbit, traveling at about 66,000 miles per hour. In an average lifetime a person travels 50 billion miles due to this orbital motion.

1885. Today Dr. William Grant of Davenport, Iowa, performed the first recorded appendectomy on a 22-year-old woman, Mary Gartside. It traditionally has been taught that the appendix is a useless "vestigial" organ left over from mankind's evolutionary past.

However, closer investigation shows that *no* part of the human body is without value and purpose. The appendix, and also our tonsils, produce antibodies which fight infection in the early stages of life. In later years these organs may become inflamed and then they can be removed safely. Physicians today are increasingly reluctant to remove any parts of the body. There is a growing appreciation of the importance and interactions of all our body components. As David sang long ago:

> I praise you because I am fearfully and wonderfully made; Your works are wonderful, I know that full well (Ps. 139:14).

JANUARY 5

1850. A large lighthouse, while under construction, was completely swept away today during a severe North Atlantic storm. Bishop Rock Lighthouse was on the Scilly Islands in southwest England. At this location some of the earth's heaviest seas frequently occur. The destroyed light tower was later rebuilt with massive granite blocks and steel reinforcement, and it still stands today. The great 1850 sea storm was a reminder of the awesome power of water, once used to judge the entire earth in the days of Noah.

• • • •

1982. Today a balanced treatment law was overturned in Arkansas. Ten months earlier the governor had signed a bill which permitted the teaching of creation evidence alongside evolution in Arkansas public schools. This law was immediately attacked by the American Civil Liberties Union, liberal religious groups, and science professors from across the nation. Creation representatives were greatly outnumbered and also outspent by the opposition. Students were the real losers in this decision. They were denied the opportunity to study the creation alternative to naturalism. The spiritual dimension of the creation-evolution controversy is clearly evident in court battles such as this.

1912. The idea of continental drift was first presented today at a geology conference in Germany. Meteorologist Alfred Wegener (1880–1930) described the possible fitting together of the continents, somewhat like the pieces of a large puzzle. He also noted similar rocks and fossils on widely separated coastlines. Wegener's novel ideas about seafloor spreading and continental drift were initially rejected by fellow scientists. Sixteen years later Wegener received a similar negative response at a 1928 meeting of American petroleum geologists.

JANUARY
6

New ideas are often unpopular in scientific circles. Today, however, almost all scientists agree that an original super-continent was divided into the present continents. Many creationists believe this continental separation occurred rapidly during the Genesis flood when the "fountains of the great deep burst forth" (Gen. 7:11;RSV). Small-scale motions of continents still continue today with several inches of movement occurring each year.

JANUARY
7

1610. Galileo (1564–1642) pointed his newly invented telescope at tonight's sky from Padua, Italy, and made several important discoveries. He was the first to see Saturn's rings and also the moon-like phases of the planet Venus. Galileo quickly realized that the created solar system was much more beautiful and complex than previously thought. He later wrote about his discovery of Jupiter's four major moons:

Saturn

What surpasses all wonders by far . . . is the discovery of four wandering stars [moons]. All these facts were discovered and observed by me not many days ago with the aid of a spyglass which I devised, after first being illuminated by divine Grace.

Galileo

1851. Early this morning a landmark discovery was made in science. French scientist Jean Foucault (1819–1868) had constructed a pendulum in his cellar. Watching closely, he noticed that the swinging pendulum slowly changed its direction of swing. Foucault correctly concluded that he was observing the entire earth rotate beneath the pendulum.

Foucault's pendulum, duplicated today in many science museums, remains the simplest demonstration that the earth rotates once each 24 hours.

Foucault went on to invent the gyroscope, used today in aircraft and space probes. A nonbeliever most of his life, Foucault finally gave honor to his Creator during an illness that took his life at age 48.

Pendulum clock

JANUARY 9

1960. Construction of the giant Aswan Dam across Egypt's Nile River began today. This massive project was completed 11 years later. Lake Nasser formed behind the dam, requiring the relocation of one hundred thousand people and also several ancient Egyptian temple complexes.

Large-scale benefits and several serious problems have followed the dam construction. Flooding of the Nile River is now controlled, but land fertility suffers as a result. Disease parasites also have multiplied greatly in Lake Nasser, afflicting millions of Egyptian citizens. Such large-scale building projects always have many profound effects. Creation details are closely interrelated and any alteration affects many other details in unexpected ways.

JANUARY 10

1946. Today the first radar signal was beamed upward toward the moon by the U.S. Army Signal Corps. This beam was reflected from the moon's surface back to earth. The round-trip travel time for the signal, traveling at light speed, was about 2.6 seconds. This measurement accurately gave the earth-moon distance, which varies between 221,600 and 252,950 miles.

Similar radar signals were later used to accurately measure the distances to nearby planets. For the faraway stars, however, other distance methods are needed since a radar beam would be completely lost in the depths of space.

The vast distance scale of space objects shows the unfathomable majesty of the creation.

1672. Isaac Newton was given full membership in the British Royal Society today at age 30. The occasion was Newton's invention of the reflecting telescope. All large telescopes built today are reflectors which use a concave mirror to gather and focus light. Newton wrote with a humble spirit:

Sir Isaac Newton

I shall endeavor to testify my gratitude by communicating what my poor and solitary endeavors can effect towards promoting the Society.

Newton was perhaps the greatest scientist of all time. He also believed firmly in the Creator and in the inspiration of Scripture. Newton's theological writings, especially concerning prophecy, outnumber his scientific papers (see March 20).

1733. America's first public museum was opened today in Charleston, South Carolina. This museum today includes many unique items including a life-size replica of a Civil War submarine. Museums display the art, culture, and sense of history that belong to mankind alone, created in God's image.

In contrast, the animal world has no obvious sense of history. In spite of numerous evolutionary exhibits, museums generally are excellent places to observe the created details of nature and known history.

1888. The National Geographic Society today was founded by John Wesley Powell and friends. The original purpose was "for the increase and diffusion of geographic knowledge." This goal has been carried out admirably. Unfortunately, the society's publications  and television programs also attempt to promote evolution at every opportunity. When one reads "between the lines," however, it is found that all research is truly creation research. It is the improper interpretation of data which leads to naturalism.

Past Society president Alexander Graham Bell once described geography as the study of "the world and all that is in it," taking the phrase from Psalm 89:11.

• • • •

1929. The American Humanist Society was established today in Hollywood, California. Its stated goal was to "humanize religion, disseminate science, stimulate thought, and promote good will." Unfortunately the group has vigorously opposed conservative Christianity and creation in particular, betraying its original purpose. A true humanist in the positive sense is one concerned with the freedom and welfare of others.

JANUARY 13

1873. An American trademark was registered today for celluloid, the main component of photographic film. John Hyatt of New York made this new form of plastic by mixing cellulose nitrate and camphor, both vegetable products. Today we are surrounded by countless useful forms of plastic. Just look around and count the many nearby plastic items. The potential for this useful material was built into the original creation for our eventual benefit.

• • • •

1890. English geologist Arthur Holmes (1890–1965) was born today. He was one of the first researchers to use the radiometric method of rock dating, devised in 1911. Holmes arrived at an earth age of a few million years. This figure was greatly increased in the following decades. However, the absolute dating of the past is a difficult problem. Many creation scientists caution that radiometric dating is uncertain and error-prone. As the only fundamental method for dating rocks, radiometric dating may be greatly over-emphasized.

1784. The personal journal of British scientist Henry Cavendish (1731–1810) shows that he performed important experiments today to probe the nature of water. Cavendish ignited hydrogen gas and found that it readily combined with oxygen to form drops of water. Water was thus seen to consist of these two gases, hydrogen and oxygen. Abundant on earth and essential to life, liquid water actually is a rare material in space (see May 2).

In this engraving from 1747, Henry Cavendish and other investigators conduct an experiment to determine the speed of electricity. On the Thames River, workers string cable across the water. An electric pulse will be sent from one side to the other while the scientists measure the elapsed time.

JANUARY 16

1786. Today the state of Virginia adopted a freedom of religion statute, drafted by Thomas Jefferson. It forbade religious discrimination, and any government requirement to support a particular church. This law later became the model for the First Amendment to the U.S. Constitution which states, "Congress shall make no law respecting the establishment of religion, or prohibiting the free exercise thereof. . . ." Forgetting this last phrase, the First Amendment in recent years has been used improperly to banish religion entirely from public schools and buildings.

1455. Johann Gutenberg (1400–1468?) was honored today with a pension for services to his community of Mainz, Germany. Gutenberg earlier had invented the first printing press with movable type. This press remained the standard form of printing for the next  four centuries. The first book published was the Gutenberg Bible in 1455. It was printed in three volumes, and 40 copies still exist today. Gutenberg's printing press placed Scripture in the hands of the common people. The second book published was a psalter, or hymnal, used for worship.

Gutenburg and his printing press.

1778. English navigator Captain James Cook (1728–1779) today discovered Hawaii, which he called the Sandwich Islands. These beautiful islands actually are the tops of submerged volcanic mountains. Their subtropical climate supports a great variety of plants and wildlife. Mark Twain called Hawaii the "loveliest fleet of islands that lies anchored in any ocean." The Hawaiian Islands may give us a glimpse of what much of the pre-flood tropical earth resembled, during the time from Adam to Noah.

• • • •

1840. Today the first science journal was produced on an electric printing press. The periodical was called *The Electro-Magnetic and Mechanic Intel-*

Captain James Cook

ligence. Over the years many thousands of science journals have appeared. There are now about one million science articles published each year worldwide. This amounts to a new article being written every three seconds, day and night, year around. Much of this specialized technical material is read by very few scholars. The flood of scientific information reveals the many details learned about the creation. However, the end of knowledge is nowhere in sight. Every scientific question that is answered leads to several new questions at a deeper level of understanding. Science specialists today know "more and more about less and less."

JANUARY
19

1920. The American Civil Liberties Union (ACLU) began today, led by labor activist Roger Baldwin. The original intent was to defend personal liberties, including freedom of speech. The ACLU first became widely known at the Scopes trial in 1925. There the ACLU lawyers helped defend the teaching of evolution in public schools. Over the years the ACLU has supported some good causes, but also many questionable ones. The group has not supported the freedom to teach creation in the public school classroom, a glaring inconsistency in the original ACLU goal of freedom of speech for everyone.

In astrology, birthdays during January 20 to February 19 are placed under the horoscope sign of Aquarius. Many people follow newspaper horoscopes to determine future personal events. In truth, however, astrology is wasteful of both time and money. It may also become harmful as an addiction. Star constellations actually have no effect on our destiny. Furthermore, the assigned astrology signs are completely outdated. Due to the earth's precession, a slow change in the direction of earth's rotation axis, no person actually is born under the sign which newspapers typically list. Horoscopes are therefore meaningless. The practice of astrology is warned against throughout Scripture (Deut. 4:19; 2 Kings 23:5; Isa. 47:13).

1979. Neptune became the outermost solar system planet this week, remaining so for the following two decades. Planet Pluto has a highly elliptical orbit which occasionally causes it to cross inside Neptune's orbit, as occurred in 1979. In contrast, the earth's solar orbit is much more circular and stable. If the earth's orbit was elongated like that of Pluto, drastic seasonal temperature changes would make life impossible. The unending variety within the solar system shows the exquisite design of the earth for our comfort and survival.

JANUARY 22

1973. The U.S. Supreme Court made a very controversial ruling today. In a Texas case called "Roe versus Wade," the court legalized abortions nationwide during the first six months of pregnancy. In the following years, untold millions of defenseless babies have been aborted. The tragedy continues, day by day, as the miracle of new life is ravaged for personal convenience.

JANUARY 23

1892. A nova or exploding star was observed tonight by Scottish observer T.D. Anderson. A dim star suddenly flared greatly in its light output. At its brightest the nova produced the light of 25,000 suns. The star's light spectrum also showed that gases from the star were moving outward at over 600 miles per second. Nova Aurigae is now known as the first well-observed nova of modern times. Within two months the nova had faded away. This dying process of stars shows that the present universe is slowly winding down. Hebrews 1:11 declares that the heavens wear out like a garment, just as we continually observe in the night sky.

• • • •

1960. An underwater vehicle called *Trieste* descended to the deepest part of the ocean today. With two researchers on board the submersible dropped 35,800 feet into the Mariana Trench, just off Guam in the western Pacific Ocean. The descent took nearly five hours. Very little is known about this remote undersea world. The deep sea trench was found to hold fascinating sea creatures, some that glow like fireflies. The Creator has blessed every part of earth with life in abundance, including the lowest depths of the sea. Long ago Job was asked by God, "Have you . . . walked in the recesses of the deep?" (Job 38:16).

1848. Today gold was discovered at the sawmill of John Sutter, near Coloma in northern California. This exciting news led to the great gold rush of 1849, with 80,000 prospectors eventually moving west. The rare element gold was created with many unique and useful properties. For example, it does not rust, tarnish, or corrode. The metal is also extremely malleable: One ounce of gold can be stretched into a fine wire 50 miles long. Gold is one of the best conductors of electricity. There are traces of gold inside most watches, calculators, and computers. Gold was created to be useful to mankind for decoration, currency, medicine, and technology.

• • • •

1986. Miranda, a moon of Uranus, was photographed today by the Voyager 2 space probe. A complex surface was found, including long parallel ridges which look somewhat like plowed furrows. There is also a large checkmark feature on the moon's surface, 100 miles in size. Because of its markings, Miranda is perhaps the most

The Voyager 2 *space probe.*

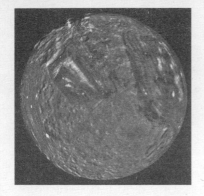

Miranda

poorly understood moon in the solar system. Space discoveries reveal a creation which is complex beyond imagination.

1839. W. Talbot produced the first photographic negative today. Two months later, artist Louis Daguerre perfected the process for producing a silver image on a copper plate. These early photographs are now called daguerreotypes.
Metal plates were eventually replaced by paper. Photography has provided a permanent record of the beauties of creation.

JANUARY
25

A daguerreotype.

1697. James Bernoulli had recently challenged his fellow scientists to solve the "brachistrone problem." This involved the complex motion of an object which falls between two different levels. A six-month time limit was placed on solving the difficult problem. Isaac Newton heard about the problem on this day and easily solved it before going to bed! He sent an unsigned solution to Bernoulli who said, "We recognize the lion by his claws." Newton, a creationist, was greatly blessed with deep insights into nature.

• • • •

1926. For the first time today, J.L. Baird demonstrated television images in London. Ever since, this invention has been a mixed blessing in many homes worldwide. Pictures give viewers a close look at faraway corners of the creation, but television also steals valuable time and exposes many people to unhealthy material content.

Although not the only one involved with the invention of television, John Baird made it a reality.

1880. Thomas Edison patented his electric incandescent light bulb today. Newspapers carried the headline "Giving Light to the World." Edison had tried nearly every

imaginable material for his glowing filament, but each burned out quickly. He wrote, "I tested no fewer than 6,000 vegetable growths, and ransacked the world for the most suitable filament material." His success finally came with a charred length of cotton thread. The first such bulb burned with a feeble red light for about 13 hours. In contrast, God spoke permanent light into existence in Genesis 1:3 by His mighty word.

The first commercial bulb.

1986. Today the space shuttle *Challenger* exploded, moments after liftoff from Florida. All seven astronauts on board were tragically killed. Later investigations found that NASA had overlooked several basic safety concerns for shuttle launches. This disaster reminds us that space technol-

The Challenger *starts to explode.*

ogy remains uncertain and imperfect. The exploration of space carries special risks. The space shuttle rides a pillar of flame 60 stories long, and it travels at 17,000 miles per hour. Just 19 years earlier (January 27, 1967) an *Apollo I* fire on the launch pad tragically killed the three pioneer astronauts Virgil Grissom, Edward White, and Roger Chaffee.

1929. The first seeing-eye dog organization began today in America. These guide dogs are of great help in leading and protecting their blind masters. Dogs were first used in Germany during World War I to aid blind veterans. German shepherds are most widely used as guide dogs because of their loyalty and their ability to learn quickly. The animal world is a blessing to mankind in many ways, including guidance for those in need.

1883. The first photograph of the Orion nebula was taken this evening. It has been followed by many thousands of similar pictures. The Orion nebula is a well-known region of dust and gas that is visible to the unaided eye during December to March, located in the constellation called Orion the Hunter.

Astronomers sometimes call the Orion nebula a stellar nursery where new stars are assumed to be slowly forming. However, this cloud may instead be original gaseous material from the creation event, or else debris from exploded stars.

1862. Tonight astronomer Alvan Clark turned his telescope toward the bright star Sirius. He noticed a tiny, bright spot near the star, now called Sirius B. This companion, a hundred times smaller than an average star, is called a white dwarf. There are indications that

Sirus B may have collapsed to its small size from a larger star as recently as 1,000 years ago. Stars can indeed change in nature as their fuel is exhausted. However, typical stellar evolution models only allow for such changes over an extremely long time span. Sirius B indicates that stars may age much faster than the computer models assume.

• • • •

1958. This date marks the launch of the first U.S. satellite, *Explorer I*. It soon discovered the Van Allen radiation belt that surrounds the earth. This satellite has been followed by thousands of others. The created laws of gravity and circular motion make satellites possible. However, all of our artificial satellites are temporary and fall back to earth sooner or later. Earth's only permanent satellite is the created moon, made on the fourth day of the creation week.

1871. This week the Cardiff Giant was revealed as a hoax. Two cousins had carved a gypsum statue of a ten-foot man, then they claimed to have discovered it as buried petrified remains near Cardiff, New York. Part of their motivation was to ridicule the reference to "giants in the earth" found in Genesis 6:4. Thousands of people eventually paid to see this fake fossil. Even some experts were fooled into believing the Cardiff Giant was either a

Illustration of the Cardiff Giant.

fossil man or an ancient statue. Three years passed before it was realized that the giant had been carved and artificially aged with ink and sulfuric acid. The Cardiff Giant story is largely forgotten today, while the Book of Genesis still stands true.

Ground Hog Day annually occurs on this date about midway through the winter season. The shadow of this furry creature is said to be a predictor of future weather. In truth, of course, neither ground hogs nor the most sophisticated weather equipment can precisely predict the weather several weeks in advance. Only the Creator fully understands and directs the complex weather components of His world.

1832. As composer Samuel Smith told the story, the song titled "America," or "My Country, 'Tis of Thee," was written "one dismal day in February." At age 24 Samuel picked up a scrap of waste paper and wrote out the verses within half an hour. The melody was carried over from the English tune "God Save the King." The patriotic words of "America" describe how creation itself clearly proclaims the joys of freedom:

> I love thy rocks and rills,
> thy woods with templed hills.
>
> Long may our land be bright
> with freedom's holy light.
>
> Protect us by thy might,
> Great God, our King.

1974. Headlines today claimed that a chimpanzee had learned to talk. Named Nim Chimsky, the animal was taught to sign simple words with motions at two months of age. There have been extensive research efforts to communicate in this way with animals, but the results have been limited.

FEBRUARY 4

   Animals indeed can be taught to respond to simple commands, but many experts refuse to define these motions as actual language. Complex language is one of many abilities that clearly sets mankind apart from the animal world. We have been created in God's image, with charge *over* the animal world.

FEBRUARY 5

1631. Today minister Roger Williams (1603–1683) and his wife arrived in Boston. He established religious freedom as the law in Rhode Island, the colony he founded. Rhode Island soon became a safe haven for Anabaptists, Quakers, and others whose beliefs otherwise were denied public expression.

The freedom of religion that America enjoys today was greatly encouraged by Roger Williams. He also learned the language of local Indians and won their trust as he shared the gospel in their own tongue.

1933. The highest sea wave ever observed occurred today near Manila in the Philippines, measuring 112 feet high (34 meters). This giant wave was not a tidal wave or tsunami. Instead, it was generated by the strong winds of a Pacific hurricane. Such violent storms show the immense power of the oceans.

FEBRUARY
6

Mankind remains unable to control the fury of the vast seas. Fortunately, there has been established a shoreline boundary to limit the extent of the sea (Ps. 104:9).

FEBRUARY
7

1996. An important announcement was made by physicists this week. They found evidence that the smallest known particle, the quark, was made up of still smaller components. This was quite upsetting to experts who thought that quarks were the ultimate building blocks of nature. However, further structure within quarks should be of little surprise. Just as outer space is complex and without any visible limit, so is the inner space of atoms. All of creation declares God's great glory, extending from the immense galaxies to the smallest subatomic particles.

FEBRUARY 8

1693. The College of William and Mary was the second college founded in the United States, after Harvard. William and Mary was chartered today in Williamsburg, Virginia. The founders stated three original purposes for the school. *First*, the youth of Virginia should be well-educated for learning and good morals. *Second*, the school should supply good ministers to Virginia. *Third*, the Indians of America should have an opportunity at the school to be instructed in Christianity. Many older schools in the United States began with similar Christian ideals in mind.

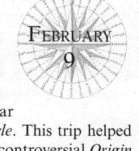

FEBRUARY 9

1809. Charles Darwin (1809–1882) was born today, just three days before the birth of Abraham Lincoln. Famous as a scientist and author, Darwin had no professional training in biology. However he enjoyed the outdoors and was selected as a naturalist on the five-year world voyage aboard the H.M.S. *Beagle*. This trip helped shape his evolutionary views. Darwin's controversial *Origin of Species* appeared 28 years after the voyage was completed. The ideas in Darwin's book have turned generations of people away from biblical creation. One might reflect on the respective legacies left by the contemporaries Charles Darwin and Abraham Lincoln.

FEBRUARY 10

1996. History was made today during a game of chess. Gary Kasparov, possibly the best chess player of all time, competed with an IBM computer called *Deep Blue* and lost. The computer was programmed to evaluate 200 million different chess positions every second. In this way it calculated every single possibility on the board within the next 10–15 moves. After losing initially, Kasparov won the following games to take the match. With his experience, pattern recognition, and intuition, Kasparov could actually see 20 moves ahead on the chessboard. The very best computers of today are still no match for the created human mind.

1847. This is Thomas Edison's birthday. He was home-schooled by his mother and largely self-taught in his technical abilities. Edison (1847–1931) earned 1,093 patents for his inventions, the most ever obtained by one person. In 1895 Edison wrote, "Nature and science both affirm [God's] existence, and where the layman believes, the man of science knows." In 1910 however, he wrote the opposite, "There is no supernatural. All there is can be explained along material lines." The troubling question remains: What negative experience occurred in Thomas Edison's later life to cause his rejection of the Creator?

1937. This week a patent was granted for the synthetic fiber called nylon. Research chemist Wallace Carothers from DuPont Corporation first made this useful polymer. Nylon is found today in clothing, strings for tennis rackets, bristles for toothbrushes, surgical sutures, and in thousands of other products. Nylon is made using the simple materials coal, water, and air. The Creator has built a host of such useful products into nature, many of which still await discovery. Incidentally, spider webs are stronger than nylon fibers or even steel fibers of the same size. Spiders seem to perform this feat using just two raw materials, water and air, in spinning their silk strands.

1633. Italian astronomer Galileo Galilei arrived in Rome today. He was brought to trial for promoting the heliocentric belief that the earth circles the sun. This event is often used to denigrate religion as being old fashioned and earth-centered. However the real problem in Galileo's day was an unhealthy alliance between science authorities and the Catholic Church. Both groups blindly supported geocentricism and both were responsible for the ill treatment of Galileo. The Bible does not teach geocentricism.

FEBRUARY
13

Galileo demonstrates the telescope.

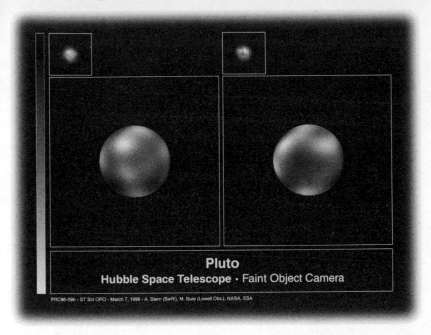

Pluto, in a Hubble Space Telescope image.

FEBRUARY 14

1930. This week Clyde W. Tombaugh (1906–1997) discovered the ninth solar system planet, Pluto, on photographs taken earlier. Others had overlooked the evidence of this dim wandering speck of light. The announcement was delayed until March 13, the anniversary of Percival Lowell's birth. Lowell had earlier predicted Pluto's existence from its observed gravity pull on planet Neptune. Pluto circles the sun at an average distance of 3.7 billion miles, 40 times farther outward from the sun than the earth. This small planet takes 249 years to complete just one orbit around the sun. The temperature on Pluto remains near -380°F (-230°C). Such extreme space conditions should increase our appreciation of planet Earth and its preparation for life.

1977. Three scientists descended 1.5 miles beneath the Pacific Ocean today aboard the submersible *Alvin*. They  were surprised to find abundant life near hydrothermal vents on the seafloor. Some of these "black smoker" vents are a dozen stories tall and emit clouds of minerals and water heated to 750⁰ F (400⁰ C). Giant mussels, clams, tube worms, fish, and bacteria also thrive nearby in spite of total darkness and enormous water pressure. Heat and chemicals from within the earth provide the energy and nutrients for the deep-sea life. Some evolutionists have suggested that life first originated near these vents. Actually this unexpected deep ocean oasis shows the diversity of life which was created everywhere on the earth at its origin. On the fifth day of creation God said, "Let the water teem with living creatures" (Gen. 1:20). More recently, valuable minerals, including gold, also have been found near the undersea vents.

 1905. The Esperanto Club was organized today in Boston. Members were dedicated to introducing a single, universal language to the world. The idea originally came from Lazarus Zamenhof (1859-1917), a Russian physician. Esperanto means "one who hopes." The new vocabulary was designed to unite features of all the languages of the world. Two versions of the New Testament were eventually produced in Esperanto. In spite of much effort and many international meetings, Esperanto is largely an unknown language today. The world will indeed adopt a single language someday according to Zephaniah 3:9, but it will be by the Creator's direction instead of man's.

1600. Giordano Bruno was burned at the stake in Rome on this date. Like astronomer Galileo, he had promoted the heliocentric idea that the earth circles the sun. He also claimed, correctly, that the stars were distant suns. The science and church leaders of his day did not tolerate such views. Their trust was in a geocentric, unmoving earth. Four centuries ago, "scientific heresy" was a dangerous practice (see February 13).

(see February 13)

FEBRUARY 17

. . . .

According to Genesis 7:11, the great flood began today when Noah was 600 years of age, "on the seventeenth day of the second month." On this day the fountains of the great deep broke forth, and also the windows of heaven were opened. A world that had turned its back on God and gone wild was destroyed, except for the precious animal and human life on board the ark. God is very patient toward mankind, but judgment day surely comes eventually.

FEBRUARY 18

1913. Today Frederick Soddy first used the term *isotope* to describe atoms of the same element that have slightly different masses. Thus, we have carbon-14, cobalt-60, etc. The mass differences result from varying numbers of neutrons within the atomic nucleus. Each of the 112 known elements has several isotopes. The known total number of these isotopes is over one thousand. Some are used as tracers in medicine, and many others have technological applications. Each isotope has its own properties and usefulness to mankind.

1671. Isaac Newton today published a paper which explained the formation of rainbows. He had calculated the multiple reflections and refractions of light through raindrops which produce the beautiful spectrum of colors in the sky. The rainbow is described in Genesis 9:13 as a visible promise of no further worldwide judgment by water. Isaac Newton's scientific explanation does not diminish the beautiful rainbow symbol of God's care.

FEBRUARY 19

FEBRUARY 20

1943. A Mexican farmer was busy plowing his cornfield today. Looking back he was surprised to see smoke rising from a furrow. A volcano had suddenly begun in his cornfield! The frightened farmer probably thought he had fractured the earth itself. Within days there was a 1,000-foot cone of debris, with hot fragments erupting 3,300 feet high. The village of Paricutin was slowly buried completely in ash except for the church steeple. The resulting cinder cone lies dormant today west of Mexico City.

Volcanoes are a reminder of the incredible heat energy stored within the earth, directly beneath our feet.

1902. The first modern brain surgery in the United States was performed successfully today on a patient by Dr. Harvey Cushing.

The human brain remains poorly understood because it is complex far

FEBRUARY 21

beyond any computer ever designed. It is found that our minds store material at parallel sites. This means that part of the brain can be damaged or removed, yet overall, detailed memory still remains. Our brains may well be the ultimate example of created design in the entire physical universe.

FEBRUARY 22

1984. A young boy touched his mother for the first time today, since his birth. "David" from Houston had spent most of his life inside a large plastic bubble because he totally lacked immunity to disease germs. Now at age 12 David needed a bone-marrow transplant, so his plastic shield was removed. His rare condition showed the critical importance of the body's defense mechanisms against infection. Sadly, David died just 15 days later.

1929. The first patient was treated today by diathermy in Schenectady, New York. Diathermy involves exposure to high frequency electric currents. The medical technique is found to increase blood flow and reduce inflammation. The human body itself produces many electrical signals within its nerves. These small electric currents regulate the processes of life. The frequencies used in diathermy provide internal heating without affecting the life-sustaining internal currents.

FEBRUARY 23

We do not fully understand electricity but our bodies have been created to use electric signals continually.

1987. Early this morning an Australian astronomer noticed a new light resulting from the explosion of a faraway star. It was in the Large Magellan Cloud, a neighboring galaxy about 200,000 light years distant and visible in the Southern Hemisphere sky. This does *not* mean that the universe is 200,000 years old; distance and time are not equivalent. The universe is vast in size while at the same time it can be young in age. The 1987 discovery was the first detailed supernova observed since 1604.

Supernovae are especially violent star explosions. At their peak these displays may glow with the light of 100 million suns. Supernovae dramatically illustrate the aging of the universe according to the Second Law of Thermodynamics.

1751. The first trained monkey was exhibited in the United States today, in New York City. For an admission of one cent, people could watch the monkey dance, clap his hands, and generally act silly.

Over the years monkeys have been a popular attraction in zoos. Monkey behavior and facial features are somewhat similar to people, and this is sometimes mistaken as evidence for our evolutionary past. In truth, of course, there are great differences between people and animals, including monkeys. Animals have no sense of history, and their actions are determined mainly by programmed instinct. Any physical similarities between living creatures show the mark of the common Creator, not a common ancestor.

1919. The Grand Canyon of Arizona was declared a national park today. The park portion of this immense gorge is 18 miles wide, 1 mile deep, and 56 miles long. It is usually assumed that the Colorado River eroded the entire canyon over eons of time. Instead, however, the Grand Canyon is a majestic monument to vast flooding. Following the Genesis flood, much water remained trapped in western lakes. Probably the eventual breaking of a natural ice dam caused large-scale, catastophic flooding through the Grand Canyon area. Rapid erosion then occurred on a colossal scale in a short time.

1932. An article in today's issue of *Nature* magazine announced the discovery of the neutron. British scientist James Chadwick (1891–1974) had detected this tiny component of matter during collision experiments between subatomic particles.

The neutron is one of three basic atomic particles, along with protons and electrons. From these three particles all the elements in the universe are constructed. The Creator formed endless variety in nature using just these three building blocks.

• • • •

1997. British scientists today announced in *Nature* that they had successfully cloned an adult sheep. This technique gives offspring which are genetically identical to the parent. Genetic engineering holds great potential for either good or evil. Many diseases of mankind, animals, and plants may be genetically eliminated. However, genetic control of human offspring could also be used for evil purposes. One wonders how far the Creator will permit genetic manipulation to progress.

• • • •

According to Genesis 8:14 Noah and his family left the ark today, a year and ten days after they had boarded (see February 17). This verse states that the earth was dry by the 27th day of the second month. A very different world greeted Noah's family at this time. Flood evidence was everywhere, and the earth's seasons probably became more evident. People were now permitted to eat meat (Gen. 9:3), and life spans rapidly decreased from preflood times. The world now entered an entirely new phase of history.

A port on the Amazon River at Leticia, Colombia, from an airplane.

FEBRUARY
28

1500. Around this date the Italian explorers Ojeda and Vespucci discovered the mouth of the mighty Amazon River. This vast river is 4,000 miles long, and is about 100 miles wide in northern Brazil where it empties into the Atlantic Ocean. The Amazon discharges 15 million gallons of water each second, which is 15 times as much as the Mississippi River.

This drainage system for the vast South American rain forest shows the magnitude of the earth's unique hydrologic cycle. The circulating moisture cleans the air, waters the earth, and recharges the ground water supply. There is nothing else to compare with the water cycle in the solar system, nor probably in the entire universe.

45 B.C. Leap year was first added to the calendar this year during the reign of Julius Caesar. The extra day is  needed because, in addition to the 365 rotations of the earth during each year, there is an extra partial rotation. It is not exactly an extra quarter day, however, so leap year must occasionally be omitted. Leap year is added to century years only when they are divisible by 400. The years 1900 and 2100 are not leap years, while 2000 and 2400 are. Perhaps the Creator established a non-exact number of days in the year to show us the complexity of time measurement.

 1872. Congress today authorized the Yellowstone area of Wyoming, Montana, and Idaho as our nation's first national park. President Ulysses S. Grant set aside 2.2 million acres "for the benefit and enjoyment of the people." It includes 10,000 hot springs, 200 geysers, and majestic scenery. Exactly 27 years later in 1899, Mount Rainier National Park was also dedicated. Establishing land for public enjoyment has become a model for many other nations. In our technological age, these parks provide a much-needed opportunity to experience the outdoor creation.

• • • •

1896. French scientist Henri Becquerel (1852–1908) discovered natural radioactivity today. Earlier he had placed a sample of pitchblende, a form of natural uranium, in a desk drawer. A wrapped package of photographic film was left on top of the desk. Today while developing the film by

chance, he found that it had been exposed. Radiation produced by the uranium had penetrated the desktop and altered the film. Radiation is an invisible part of the creation with great energy and with potential for useful applications.

Henri Becquerel

MARCH 2

1972. This evening the U.S. *Pioneer 10* spacecraft began its long journey into deep space. Eleven years later it became the first space probe to leave the solar system, traveling at its continuous speed of 28,000 miles per hour, or one half-million miles each day. *Pioneer 10* is now more than 7 billion miles from earth and its weak radio signal has faded away. A plaque attached to *Pioneer*'s side shows a couple waving. The stated hope is that a few hundred thousand years from now, distant space aliens may capture the *Pioneer* probe and realize that we earthlings are friendly. This search for life in space forgets that the Creator of the universe has already contacted us through His Son and His Word.

MARCH 3

1899. A collision between two British ships occurred today, the *East Goodwin* and a steamer. Instantly from across the water came a distress call by wireless radio. It was one of the first uses of the radio, invented just months earlier by the Italian physicist Guglielmo Marconi (1874–1937). Lifeboats rushed to the scene and rescued the passengers and crew. Today the world is tied together by millions of radio and telephone signals. This communication is an important gift from the Creator. Radio waves follow the curvature of the earth because of atmospheric reflection, connecting far-distant locations. Satellites also provide near-instant contact, a special blessing for remote missionary stations.

Marconi and his wireless radio.

1675. Today astronomer John Flamsteed was appointed the first director of the Greenwich Observatory in England. This observatory later became the origin point for the longitude lines which circle the earth. Greenwich, England, is on the prime meridian at zero degrees longitude. This grid of latitude and longitude lines greatly helps the navigation and mapping of our wide world. The Greenwich Observatory was closed in 1998, after 323 years of operation.

MARCH
4

MARCH 5

1827. Pierre-Simon Laplace (1749–1827) drew his last breath today and spoke these final words: "Man follows only phantoms." Laplace was a famous French mathematician and scientist. In his book *Celestial Mechanics* he popularized the Nebular Hypothesis for the origin of the solar system. In this view the sun and planets long ago formed spontaneously from contracting gas clouds in space. Laplace once met with Napoleon who remarked, "You have written this large book on the system of the universe, and have never even mentioned its Creator." Author Laplace replied, "Sir, I had no need of that hypothesis." Laplace was an atheist who did his best to remove the Creator from science. This unsatisfying approach to life is reflected in his final sad words of despair.

MARCH 6

1869. The periodic table that is displayed in many science classrooms was first published today. Russian chemist and teacher Dmitri Mendeleev (1834–1907) realized that the atomic elements differed sequentially in weight. His first table listed 63 elements in order of weight, and he also predicted several unknown elements to fill gaps which appeared in the table. Several of these additional elements were soon found including gallium (1875), scandium (1879), and germanium (1885). In Mendeleev's funeral procession, his appreciative students carried a large banner displaying the periodic table. This table clearly demonstrates the orderliness of creation. It also shows the Lord's ability to construct many different elements using just three basic particles that make up all atoms: electrons, protons, and neutrons.

MARCH 7

1982. Many people were frightened this month by the news that the world would soon end. Two British scientists predicted that all nine of the solar system planets were about to line up. This would momentarily place the planets in a straight line, outward from the sun. Their combined gravity effect was then predicted to completely pull the earth out of shape and trigger widespread earthquakes. The dire story was called the Jupiter Effect, named for the largest planet. In truth the planets did not line up completely, and their combined gravity pull on the earth is negligible regardless. The Jupiter Effect was simply not true. Only the Creator knows the calendar details for the earth's future. Believers look forward to the new heavens and earth that He has planned, and leave the future in His hands.

Johannes Kepler

MARCH 8

1618. Today astronomer Johannes Kepler (1571–1630) discovered that the planets orbit the sun with elliptical paths. This conclusion involved years of observations and analyzing data, long before computers or calculators were available. Kepler also found the "Harmonic Law" that describes how planet orbit times lengthen with their increasing distance from the sun. His testimony of discovery is recorded in a statement made on this special day: "God has passed before me in the grandeur of His ways."

MARCH 9

1975. Work officially began on the Alaskan oil pipeline today. A few years earlier vast oil reserves had been discovered beneath the waters of the Arctic Ocean on Alaska's North Slope. Alaska currently supplies about 20 percent of U.S. domestic oil. Coal, oil, and natural gas are thought to result largely from buried vegetation. Much of this fossil fuel surely resulted from the rapid burial of immense amounts of tropical biomass during the Genesis flood.

MARCH 10

1748. A life was changed forever on this date. John Newton (1725–1807) was the young captain of a slave ship traveling between North Africa and England. He held little regard for the lives of others.

During a storm which threatened to sink his ship, Newton read from Thomas a Kempis' book *Imitation of Christ* (1462). The written message convicted Newton of his cruel occupation and his need for a personal Savior.

In future years Newton became a pastor and author of hundreds of hymns. One well-known example, *Amazing*

Grace, describes the timeless future when the new heavens and earth are established:

> When we've been there ten thousand years,
> Bright shining as the sun,
> We've no less days to sing God's praise
> Than when we'd first begun.

John Newton wrote his own epitaph, etched on his gravestone in England:

> John Newton, clerk
> once an infidel and libertine,
> a servant of slaves in Africa,
> was by the rich mercy of our Lord and Saviour,
> Jesus Christ
> preserved, restored, pardoned,
> and appointed to preach the faith he had long
> labored to destroy.

• • • •

1876. The first complete sentence was spoken over a telephone today. The device had been invented by Alexander Graham Bell (1847–1922) and his assistant Thomas Watson, and patented three days earlier. The call simply went between rooms in Bell's Boston home. The sentence was "Mr. Watson, come here, I need you." Bell had just spilled some acid on himself, so the first telephone use was a "911 call" for help!

Telephones now instantly connect every corner of the world. This invention is a remarkable gift from God. When Bell died on August 4, 1922, all U.S. telephones fell silent for one minute to honor this great inventor.

1986. A fleet of space probes greeted Comet Halley during its most recent appearance. The European *Giotto* probe closely approached Halley today and transmitted detailed pictures back to earth. The comet was found to be irregular in shape, extremely dark in color, and its surface was punctured by jets of gas and dust spewing outward into space. Comets are active members of the created solar system. They are a solid collection of frozen chemicals which melt slightly when close to the sun. The existence of hundreds of known comets is an indication that the created earth and solar system are not ancient.

The orbit of Halley's Comet is so large that it passes by the earth once every 76 years or so.

1888. A legendary blizzard struck the northeast United States today. Weather forecasters had called for fair weather. Instead, however, several feet of snow were dumped on New York

City. As drifts reached 20 feet heights, electric wires and roofs collapsed and 400 fatalities resulted. Newspapers later described the New York situation as "knocked out . . . chaos reigned, and the proud boastful metropolis was reduced to the condition of a primitive settlement." A storm can quickly change the plans of both people and animals, as described in Job 37:7–8:

> So that all men he has made may know his work,
> he stops every man from his labour. The animals
> take cover; they remain in their dens.

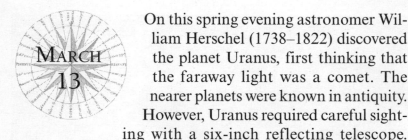

MARCH 13

On this spring evening astronomer William Herschel (1738–1822) discovered the planet Uranus, first thinking that the faraway light was a comet. The nearer planets were known in antiquity. However, Uranus required careful sighting with a six-inch reflecting telescope. Herschel later wrote, "I had gradually perused the great Volume of the Author of Nature and was now come to the page which contained the seventh Planet." Early astronomers generally showed humble respect for the Creator who revealed His universe to them.

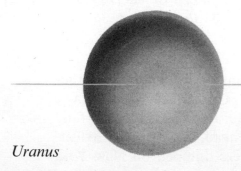

Uranus

1879. Albert Einstein (1879–1955) was an outstanding physicist thinker and this is his birthday. The Creator blessed Einstein with great insights into science, especially concerning astronomy and the relativity theory. This led to many successful predictions concerning light properties and space travel. In spite of his great intellect, however, Einstein was apparently misled by writers such as Darwin. Einstein's testimony as a young man:

Albert Einstein

Through the reading of popular scientific books I soon realized that much in the stories in the Bible could not be true.

There is clearly a vast difference between *knowledge* concerning the world and *wisdom* concerning God.

1931. The first blood bank was established today in Chicago. Hospitals worldwide are now dependent on this precious resource of life. The human body consists of billions of cells bathed in blood fluid. Some evolutionists have explored similarities between blood and seawater. They believe that life somehow began in the early oceans, and that blood still carries this saltwater chemistry. However the unique complexity of blood is shown by the existence of blood banks. Truly, the key to physical life is in the blood, exactly as stated in Leviticus 17:11 and 14.

1963. An article appeared in today's *Nature* magazine concerning a strange new type of light source discovered in deep space. Many similar light sources have now been detected, called quasars or quasi-stellar objects. Quasars hold the record as the most distant objects seen.

MARCH 16

They are thought to be the centers of certain very energetic galaxies. Tremendous light radiation is generated and emitted from them. Quasars demonstrate the unending variety and size of the created universe.

MARCH 17

A.D. 492. Saint Patrick died on this date and was buried in Ireland, his homeland. Patrick had been captured by pirates at age 16 and sold into slavery. He later became a Christian and returned to Ireland as a missionary, assisting in founding over 300 churches. On one occasion Patrick is said to have picked a shamrock and used it to illustrate the mystery of the Trinity. The three leaves represented the three persons of the Trinity — Father, Son, and Holy Spirit — and the stem was the three-in-one unity of the godhead. The Creator has indeed given us many object lessons to help our understanding of Him. Each year on Saint Patrick's birthdate there are parades and the "wearing of the green" to commemorate the patron saint of Ireland.

1952. For the first time today, a cataract patient was fitted with a plastic eye lens in Philadelphia. Cataracts involve a clouding of the lens with blurring of vision, and sometimes eventual blindness. The eye heals very quickly from surgery, and cataract removal now brings relief  to thousands of people every year. Man-made lenses, however, lack the flexible, focusing ability of our created eye lens.

Traditionally, swallows have returned to the mission at San Juan Capistrano in southern California each year on this date. These small fork-tailed birds winter in Argentina, 6,000 miles away. Then in the spring the swallows return to California over a several-week period. Bird migration in general is a wonder of creation. These tiny creatures are programmed by their Maker to tell time and direction, and also to store up sufficient energy for their amazing long-distance flights.

1727. At age 82, Isaac Newton died on this date. He was buried in London's Westminster Abbey alongside kings and queens. His marker reads, "Let

mortals rejoice that there existed such and so great an orna-
ment to the human race." Newton was a lifelong student of
the Bible. In fact, he wrote more theology than science. His
favorite Bible books were Daniel and Revelation, which con-
cern God's plans for the future.

1935. One of several great "dust bowl"
storms swept across Kansas today.
Farmers earlier had plowed the Great
Plains grasslands, hoping that "rain
would follow the plow." Instead the soil
was exposed to strong winds. Several
years of drought also added to the problem.
The vast clouds of blowing dust showed the unexpected im-
plications of modifying the environment. Many "black bliz-
zards" during this year destroyed the fields and dreams of
farmers across the Great Plains states.

The beginning of spring is always
within 1 or 2 days of this date. This
time of year is called the spring, or ver-
nal equinox. The sun appears to cross
the equator into the Northern Hemisphere where it will remain for the next
six months. As spring begins there are ex-
actly 12 hours of daylight and 12 hours of night everywhere
on earth, hence the name "equinox" with equal days and
nights. This date also marks the beginning of fall for locations south of the equator. Our seasons result from the constant 23.5° tilt of the earth's axis. Genesis 8:22 promises
that these faithful seasons will continue as long as the earth
remains.

1925. Tennessee today passed a creation law for its public schools. The Butler Act stated that "it shall be unlawful for any teacher in any of the universities, normal and all other public schools of the state which are supported in whole or in part by the public funds of  the state to teach any theory that denies the story of the Divine creation of man as taught in the Bible, and to teach instead that man has descended from a lower order of animals." Critics immediately made plans to test the law. A staged conviction under the law involved John T. Scopes (see July 24).

1989. Today the oil tanker *Exxon Valdez* struck Bligh Reef in Alaska's Prince William Sound. The resulting oil spill totaled 240,000 barrels, which coated 45 miles of pristine coastline. A multibillion dollar cleanup effort soon followed. Researchers also noticed that the land and water worked to purify themselves by dilution and dispersion of the oil. Oil-eating bacteria were also active participants in restoring the area. The Creator has placed many built-in safety mechanisms in nature to restore and maintain its health.

1989. Headlines this week reported that two Utah researchers had harnessed nuclear fusion. The scientists claimed success with a simple experiment performed in their laboratory. There was great surprise since hundreds of

scientists have been studying nuclear fusion for decades with large instruments and million degree temperatures, and with very limited success. The Utah report has now been largely discredited. Nuclear fusion is thought to be the energy source of the sun and all other stars. However, scientists have had little success in controlling this process which the Creator uses daily to provide our sunshine.

MARCH 26

1953. This week Jonas Salk (1914–1995) announced his new vaccine against poliomyelitis, or polio. This serious disease especially attacks youth, and was quickly brought under control in America. School children nationwide were given the vaccine. Dr. Salk was called "the man who saved the children." Ever since the curse of Genesis 3:14–16, diseases have ravaged the earth. In His mercy the Creator has provided many tools to fight sickness.

MARCH 27

1860. On this day a U.S. patent was granted to M.L. Byrn for the corkscrew. This device works like a common wood screw but is made in a spiral or helix shape. It allows removal of a cork from a bottle without splitting the cork. The corkscrew principal has many other applications such as augers for moving grain, anchors for cables, and gears for machinery. As is true for most inventions, the corkscrew was already present in nature. Filaree is an herb whose seed is at the end of a long corkscrew tail of plant material. The seed itself has a pointed end which lodges itself in soil. A breeze then turns the spiral tail and drills the seed directly into the ground. This unique method of seed burial is a marvel of creative engineering. Its origin goes back to the third day of creation when plants were made (Gen. 1:11).

MARCH 28

1979. This morning a nuclear reactor at the Three Mile Island power plant near Middletown, Pennsylvania, malfunctioned. There were no injuries, but the partial meltdown of the reactor resulted in a two billion dollar cleanup effort. The Creator has placed an almost limitless amount of energy within atoms. Unfortunately our tapping of this nuclear energy has proved a difficult task.

On Mercury, the planet closest to the sun, today is already the last day of the year. Mercury completes a solar orbit in just 88 earth days, traveling continually at 107,000 miles per hour. This planet is dry, cratered, and constantly bombarded by deadly solar radiation. Like Mercury, all of our solar system neighbors help us appreciate the special preparation of earth for life. There is no other place like home!

MARCH 29

MARCH 30

1842. Ether was used for the first time today as an anesthetic during surgery. Dr. Crawford Long performed the operation in Jefferson, Georgia. Anesthetics are a great gift in easing human pain.

There are many such blessings, which limit the physical effects of the curse. For example, we must work by the sweat of our brow for food, but at least we do eat (Gen. 3:19). Women have pain during childbirth, but we then experience the joy of children (Gen. 3:16). Greatest of all, the present curse on nature and on mankind is only temporary for those who know the Creator.

1918. Daylight Saving Time first went into effect today in the United States. The initial goal was to make better use of the early morning light for economic efficiency during World War I. The time change initially was very unpopular and was dropped after only one year.

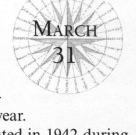

Daylight Saving Time was again instituted in 1942 during the Second World War, called "War Time," and the annual adjustment has largely remained since then. These annual time adjustments remind us how dependent we are on daily sunshine.

1948. A significant letter appeared in today's *Physical Review* journal. It was titled "The Origin of Chemical Elements." The one-page letter suggested that all elements in the universe had formed in the aftermath of a big bang explosion. This idea remains popular today in spite of serious problems with the big bang theory. The three physicist authors of the science letter have last names which sound like the Greek alphabet letters alpha, beta, and gamma. The authors were R.A. Alpher, H. Bethe, and G.

Gamow. Perhaps the letter should not be taken too seriously, since it was unintentionally published on April Fool's Day!

1798. *The Creation* is a well-known oratorio by Franz Joseph Haydn (1732–1809). It was first sung today in Vienna. The music beautifully captures the majesty and mystery of the biblical creation story. The words are taken from Scripture and also from Milton's *Paradise*

APRIL
2

Lost. One portion declares that "The heavens are telling the glory of God," from Psalm 19:1. Artistic expression can be a wonderful way to honor our Creator.

Franz Joseph Haydn

APRIL
3

1981. An amazing feat was accomplished today in athletic competition. Arnie Boldt of Saskatchewan, Canada, has only one leg. In spite of this, he was able to high jump 6 feet, 8.25 inches. He thus demonstrated an outstanding ability to compete and excel physically. The designed human body is capable of deeds thought to be nearly impossible, including Boldt's record jump.

1932. Vitamin C was first isolated and identified today by C.C. King at the University of Pittsburgh. Vitamins are organic substances essential to good nutrition. Vitamin C, also called ascorbic acid, has multiple functions in our bodies. It aids cell development in skin, cartilage, and bone. It helps heal wounds and fractures, and also prevents scurvy. The long list of essential vitamins and minerals demonstrates the close connection between created life and the food resources which the Creator makes available to sustain us.

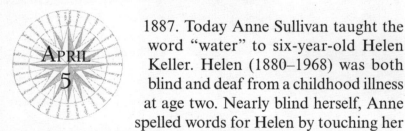

1887. Today Anne Sullivan taught the word "water" to six-year-old Helen Keller. Helen (1880–1968) was both blind and deaf from a childhood illness at age two. Nearly blind herself, Anne spelled words for Helen by touching her hand. Helen Keller later went on to become an outstanding author and educator. She graduated with honors from Radcliffe at age 24.

Helen wrote, "I have always thought it would be a blessing if each person could be blind and deaf a few days during his early adult life. Darkness would make him appreciate sight; silence would teach him the joys of sound." Anne Sullivan and Helen Keller show the great potential created within us for overcoming difficult problems in life.

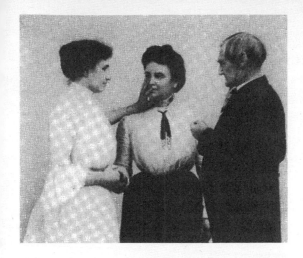

Helen Keller is noted for her work for the blind.

1909. On this day Robert Peary, Matthew Henson, and four Eskimos became the first explorers to reach the North Pole. Peary had failed in several attempts over a 15-year period. The South Pole was reached by Roald Amundsen two years later in 1911 (see December 14). In these cold polar regions the sun never climbs very high in the sky, if at all. These remote locations reveal how much we depend on the sun for daily light and warmth.

• • • •

1938. An unexpected new material was made today during chemistry research. It was a slippery plastic substance now called teflon. Bakeries were the first to use teflon-coated muffin pans; frying pans soon followed. This material is now found in rocket heat shields, fuel tanks, and also in electronics. Teflon does not exist in nature but there are somewhat similar natural materials. For example, *pitcher plants*, which grow worldwide, have hollow horn-shaped leaves with an extremely smooth inner surface. Insects that land on the inner edge quickly slide down the slippery surface and into acid secretions at the bottom. The acid is strong enough to digest the insect but does not damage the plant itself because of a natural teflon-like surface coating. Many inventions have their counterparts in the created world.

APRIL 7

1864. Chemist Louis Pasteur gave a speech today at the famous Sorbonne University in Paris. His topic concerned the spontaneous generation of

Louis Pasteur

life. Pasteur had studied vessels of water, some open to air currents and dust, and others sealed. Regarding the latter he said, "Now the liquid in this second flask will remain pure not only two days, a month, a year, but three or four years. For the experiment I am telling you about is already four years old, and the liquid remains as pure as distilled water." These early experiments refuted the spontaneous origin of life, and are still valid today. Pasteur went further and said life was one thing that "has not been given to man to produce" from raw matter. Ever since the creation, life has always come from other life. As Genesis 1 reminds us, living things reproduce after their own kinds.

APRIL
8

1812. Young Michael Faraday attended a lecture tonight presented by chemist Humphrey Davy. Although Faraday never attended school, he had learned to read and write in Sunday school and at home.

The young Faraday carefully recopied his lecture notes, had them bound, and then presented them to Humphrey Davy. Davy was impressed and soon hired Faraday as his laboratory assistant. Thus began Michael Faraday's brilliant career as a scientist. Faraday built the first electric motor. He also discovered benzene and liquefied chlorine.

Throughout his life

Michael Faraday

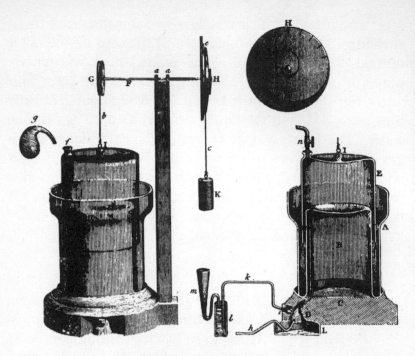

Sir Humphrey Davy's gas machine.

Faraday was a conservative Christian and belonged to a group called the Sandemanians. He also loved to share creation insights with others. Attenders described his popular, public science lectures as a worship experience.

1966. This week the cover of *Time* magazine asked the question, "Is God Dead?" This foolish idea goes back to the German philosopher Friedrich Nietzsche (1844–1900). It implies that God does not exist, and never did exist. Radical theologians gave leadership to the idea that "we must learn to get along without God." Several decades later, the "God is Dead" movement itself has largely disappeared. Nietzsche died in an insane asylum, while conservative Christianity flourishes. As David said long ago:

The fool says in his heart, "There is no God" (Ps. 14:1, 53:1).

APRIL 10

1816. Mount Tambora in Indonesia violently erupted this week, the greatest explosion in a millennium. Fifty cubic kilometers (12 cubic miles) of earth material were thrown skyward with the energy of 40,000 hydrogen bombs. The tremendous blast killed 12,000 people and threw dust high into the atmosphere. This event lowered temperatures worldwide and 1816 became the "year without a summer" in New England. Our stable climate is balanced by many factors. When changes occur such as a volcanic eruption, the weather effects are immediate and worldwide.

APRIL 11

1957. Today the Ryan X-13 Vertijet became the first aircraft to take off and land vertically, thus needing no runway. There have been several more advanced vertical-motion airplanes designed since the Vertijet. These aircraft attempt to duplicate the flying abilities of common insects and also many birds. Try to capture one of these creatures and you will quickly see their advanced flight techniques, far beyond our limited engineering capabilities. Animal flight appeared fully functional and miraculously on the fifth and sixth days of creation.

APRIL 12

1961. Soviet cosmonaut Yuri Gagarin became the first person to orbit the earth today. The trip lasted 89 minutes with a capsule speed of about 17,000 miles per hour. Russian leader Nikita Khrushchev proudly declared that man had traveled into space and had not seen God there. Someone responded that if a person steps outside his space capsule, he will meet God quickly! Gagarin actually had gone only 188 miles outward from the earth, hardly into deep space. God can be found right at home; there is no need to travel beyond the earth to locate the Creator.

1742. The first public performance of Handel's *Messiah* took place tonight in Dublin, Northern Ireland. German

APRIL 13

Composer George Frederick Handel.

composer George Frederick Handel (1695–1759) had written this oratorio during 23 days of intense work during the previous year. This music is now traditionally performed at Christmastime. The *Messiah* beautifully describes the coming of the Creator to earth two thousand years ago, and also His triumphant return, as described in Revelation 11:15:

> The kingdom of this world is become the kingdom of our Lord, and of his Christ; and he shall reign for ever and ever.

1881. Animal rights is a popular modern topic. Actually, however, it has been present for a long time. Charles Darwin wrote a letter today approving measures that would prevent unnecessary cruelty to animals in the laboratory. He added, "Physiology can make no progress if experiments on living animals are suppressed. . . . See the results obtained by Pasteur's work on the germs of contagious diseases: Will not animals be the first to profit thereby?" Darwin was correct in this balanced position on animal research. It should be permitted while avoiding any unnecessary animal suffering or mistreatment.

1912. In the early morning hours today the British luxury liner *Titanic* was lost on the fifth day of its maiden voyage. About 1,500 crew and passengers drowned in the frigid waters of the North Atlantic. The ship had hit an iceberg which split open its hull. Water is one of very few materials which floats in its frozen, solid state. This designed property makes life possible on earth. Surface ice prevents lakes and seas from freezing solidly and permanently from the bottom upward. This alternative would surely extinguish life completely on the earth.

Unfortunately, icebergs are a resulting hazard to shipping. Overall, the benefits of floating ice far outweigh the hazards to shipping.

APRIL 16

1951. This week a lecture was delivered to the British Interplanetary Society by J.B.S. Haldane (1892–1964). A world-class geneticist, Haldane said, "From the fact that there are 400,000 species of beetles on this planet, but only 8,000 species of mammals, I have concluded that the Creator, if He exists, has a special fondness for beetles, and so we might be more likely to meet them than any other type of animal on a planet which would support life." Another time Haldane was asked what nature revealed about God. His reply: "An inordinate fondness for beetles." Haldane was correct in describing the large number of beetles on earth, about 20 percent of all the known forms of life. However, Haldane's book *The Causes of Evolution* (1932) unfortunately promoted the rejection of special creation in favor of Darwinism.

1629. Today horses were first imported to the American colonies. They were delivered from Europe by the Massachusetts Bay Company for use in farming and travel. Worldwide, horses always have been of great value in easing the labor of mankind. Horse fossils exist

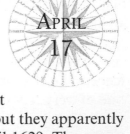

APRIL 17

in North America from preflood times, but they apparently had disappeared from the continent until 1629. The popular story of the gradual evolution of the horse from a small badger-like animal is simply not true. Neither the fossil record nor genetics supports horse evolution. Horses, along with other animal kinds, appeared supernaturally on the sixth day of the creation week. The first Biblical mention of the horse is in Genesis 49:17, during the time of Jacob, around 2000 B.C.

1867. Gregor Mendel (1822–1884) is known as the Father of Genetics. In 1857 he began garden experiments with peas which revealed the laws of heredity. Mendel carried on his research at the Monastery of St. Thomas in Austria. He found that parent plants do not simply blend characteristics in their progeny, but instead pass them on as discrete factors. Thus, Mendel correctly described the properties of genes which he called traits. Mendel published very little and his work was not recognized as important during his lifetime. A letter written today to a friend clearly expressed his patient scientific attitude: "experiments proceed slowly . . . one's interest is refreshed daily, and the care which must be given to one's wards (plants) is thus amply repaid."

1984. An article today in the British journal *Nature* suggested a new reason for the death of the dinosaurs. Perhaps there was a "death star" named *Nemesis* that periodically approaches the solar system, causing great cosmic disturbance and death to creatures upon the

earth. A subsequent search for such a star in space has failed completely. Instead of a death star, dinosaurs may well have died out because of the cooler climate which followed the

Genesis flood. It does not appear likely that the Creator periodically sends death stars to extinguish life on earth.

1940. The first electron microscope was demonstrated today in Philadelphia, by RCA, an electronics company. This instrument has a much larger magnification than ordinary microscopes which use visible light. In this new microscope a beam of electrons display wavelike properties when accelerated to high speeds. These waves are able to image very tiny objects. Electron microscopes have greatly extended our view of creation to the smallest scale possible.

1955. Today the play *Inherit the Wind* opened in New York City. This drama unfairly portrayed the 1925 Scopes evolution trial as a battle between scientific truth and Christian ignorance. A movie version of the play appeared in 1960, expressing these same, slanted sentiments. The play title comes from Proverbs 11:29, "He that troubleth his own house shall inherit the wind" (KJV). Hindsight and Scripture would suggest that it is evolutionary dogma which has unleashed a whirlwind of confusion and trouble upon society.

1864. Today Congress established the motto "In God We Trust" for the two-cent piece. A pastor had recently written to the Secretary of the Treasury concerning Civil War losses: "From my heart I have felt our national shame in disowning God as not the least of our present national disasters. . . . I suggest the recognition of the Almighty God in some form on our coins." The motto was chosen to clearly express in a few words that no nation can be strong except in the strength of God. A century later, in 1955, Congress officially mandated that all United States currency and coins shall bear the inscription "In God We Trust."

．．．．

1970. Today the first international Earth Day was celebrated by environmental groups. Millions of people around the world participated in anti-pollution demonstrations and marches. This annual event has "lost its way" in recent years as it has become more political, and controlled by financial interests. There *are* valid reasons for earth stewardship. However they are based on recognition of the earth as God's precious artwork, a much higher motive than mere self-preservation.

1977. A Japanese fishing trawler netted a strange object near New Zealand this week. It was the decaying body of a "sea monster," 32 feet long and weighing two tons. After brief study and photographs, the carcass was discarded overboard. Evidence now suggests that the animal may have been a plesiosaur-type marine reptile. However the plesiosaur is commonly thought to have died out 65 million years ago! Perhaps, instead, there are isolated communities of plesiosaur-type animals still living in the vast oceans.

APRIL
23

APRIL 24

1990. The Hubble Telescope was launched into earth orbit today aboard the space shuttle *Discovery*. This instrument initially cost $1.5 billion, weighs 12.5 tons, and carries a 95-inch parabolic mirror to gather starlight. The space telescope has explored many creation details never before seen. Planets, exploding stars, quasars, and faraway galaxies all have been photographed in detail. This telescope has also raised serious questions about natural origin theories such as the big bang.

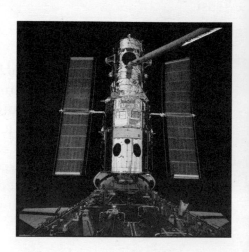

The Hubble telescope is lifted out of the space shuttle.

APRIL 25

This is the latest date on which Easter can occur. The earliest possible date for this holy day is March 22. The date for Easter is actually determined by the time of the full moon phase each spring. A complicated Easter formula was established by the church council of Nicea in A.D. 325. How appropriate to have this special day appointed by the faithful, created moon.

• • • •

1602. Scientist William Harvey today received his medical degree from the University of Padua in Italy. Harvey went on to discover the circulation of blood in living creatures. His studies clearly showed the truth of Leviticus 17:14, that the "life of every creature is its blood." Harvey published his blood circulation ideas in 1628 and then faced a long period of opposition. His work represents the beginning of modern physiology.

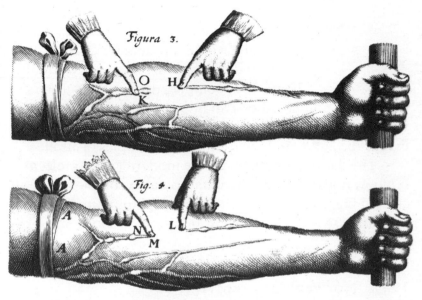

Harvey's design deduction on one-way valves in veins of the arm.

1920. Today a famous debate took place during a meeting of the U.S. National Academy of Sciences. Two astronomers discussed the size of the universe, in particular the distance to mysterious swirls of light in the night sky. Harlow Shapely took the position that they were nearby gas clouds. Herber Curtis countered that they were distant galaxies, faraway islands of stars in deep space. This debate was settled five years later when the new Mount Wilson telescope in California revealed that the swirls were indeed vast, remote galaxies (see January 1).

APRIL 27

1953. An important article appeared this week in *Nature* magazine, written by two young British scientists, James Watson and Francis Crick. They reported the structure of the DNA double helix. This complex deoxyribonucleic acid molecule is composed of two intertwining chains of atoms which encode the information for heredity. This double helix has the ability to "unzip" and make copies of itself.

The discovery opened up the modern era of molecular biology. It also showed the unfathomable complexity of all created life. Every living cell, whether plant or animal, contains the DNA helix structure, designed by God.

1947. Norwegian scientist Thor Heyerdahl and five companions departed Peru today aboard their Kon-Tiki raft, made of balsa logs and bamboo. During 101 days they sailed the Pacific Ocean currents from South America to Tahiti, a distance of 4,300 miles. Their goal was to show how ancient seafaring people may have populated remote areas of the world. Heyerdahl succeeded, perhaps similar to the worldwide dispersion of people following the Tower of Babel as described in Genesis 11:1–9.

APRIL 28

APRIL 29

1913. The common all-purpose zipper was patented today by Gideon Sudback of Sweden. One of the first uses for zippers was on snow boots. Actually the zipper structure has been present since the creation week itself. As an example, the DNA molecule replicates or copies itself by "unzipping" along its length and then reattaching both halves to new molecules.

It was announced today by John Cockcroft and Ernest Walton that the atom had been split for the first time. A particle accelerator had successfully collided protons with lithium atoms. The result was the conversion of the lithium into helium atoms. Thus it was shown that one type of atom could be converted entirely to a new atom. Many decades later, the intricacy of the atomic and nuclear worlds still baffle the understanding of researchers.

APRIL 30

• • • •

A new atomic element was discovered today. Scientists in Berkeley, California, bombarded the rare element einsteinium with atoms of helium. New atoms resulted from the collision, later named medelevium. This was the first element to be synthesized and discovered as single isolated atoms. Mendelevium is named for the Russian chemist who developed the periodic table of the elements (see March 6). All the varieties or isotopes of medelevium that have been discovered are radioactive and have only temporary lifetimes. In contrast, most of the created elements we find in nature are stable and permanent.

MAY 1

1884. Ground was broken today for Chicago's first skyscraper, a ten-story building. This construction project was later dwarfed by others including the 110-story Sears Tower (1973), Chicago's tallest building at 1,454 feet.

A strong steel substructure makes such heights possible. Worldwide construction is underway for still-higher buildings made of new metal alloys and composite materials. Eventually, mile-high buildings may literally be above the clouds, connected with enclosed walkways at upper levels.

These lofty building plans remind us of the city of New Jerusalem as described in Revelation 21:16. This future celestial city is cube-shaped, and extends 1,400 miles on each side. Such a vast size is almost beyond thinking, even for modern tower builders. The Creator will make this magnificent structure in His own way, not limited by our human engineering constraints.

MAY 2

1800. Today British scientist William Nicholson (1753–1815) used chemicals to build a primitive battery. This was long before anyone thought about readily available flashlight batteries! Nicholson passed current from his homemade battery through water and watched bubbles form. These were found to be hydrogen and oxygen gases.

He had succeeded in dissecting water into its component parts by electrolysis. Water is a precious compound created with many unusual properties that are still being studied today (see January 15).

MAY 3

1885. Henry Ward Beecher (1813-1887) began an influential series of sermons today. A preacher in New York City, Beecher was much enamored with the evolutionary ideas of his day. He taught that the enlightenment of science was nothing less than the coming of God's kingdom to earth. Science progress was thus put on an equal or higher pedestal than the Bible itself. Unfortunately this liberal view has continued since Beecher's day in many churches. Such thinking grossly underestimates the value of Scripture, and it also overestimates the value of science in answering the basic questions of life. Beecher's uncertainty in his own destiny is revealed by his final, dying words: "Now comes the mystery." A sister of Henry, Harriet Beecher Stowe, wrote the classic anti-slavery novel *Uncle Tom's Cabin* in 1852.

MAY 4

1825. British biologist Thomas Henry Huxley (1825–1895) was born today, and was the first man to call himself an *agnostic*, a term he first used in 1869. An agnostic believes that exact knowledge is limited to material objects. The spirit world is uncertain, if it exists at all. As a contentious defender of evolution, Huxley was known as "Darwin's bulldog."

Upon the death of his son, Huxley showed the despair of agnosticism in a letter to a friend: "If wife and child and name and fame were all to be lost to me one after the other . . . [I still] refuse to put faith in that which does not rest on sufficient evidence."

• • • •

1954. Earnest Hooton (1887–1954) was a leading American anthropologist and author. His obituary appeared today in the *New York World-Telegram and Sun* newspaper. The article summarized Hooton's pessimistic outlook on the development of man:

> Up to 30,000 years ago man could boast a proud evolutionary record, but since then no physical improvement has occurred. . . . Mankind is in the process of a physical and mental degeneration which is producing a resurgence of the ape within him.

Perhaps experts like Hooton themselves have contributed to the problem. They have falsely taught that man is an animal, a mere product of chance with no plan, absolute laws, or destiny. Society today bears the consequences of this philosophy of despair.

MAY 5

1816. The American Bible Society was founded today in New York City. Its purpose was "to encourage the wider circulation of the Holy Scriptures throughout the world." The Society grew out of a spiritual awakening that swept across America nearly two centuries ago. The early goal and effort of the Society was to place a Bible in every home, especially those on the American frontier.

MAY 6

1954. The four-minute mile was officially broken today. British medical student Roger Bannister ran the mile in 3 minutes 59.4 seconds during a track meet in Oxford, Ohio. In recent years this running time has been reduced below 3 minutes 45 seconds. Diet and training contribute greatly toward such outstanding athletic abilities. These achievements display the human body's wonderful design and capabilities.

1911. Ernest Rutherford publically presented his view of the atom today. He had discovered that atoms consist of a compact positive nucleus surrounded by negative orbiting electrons. Rutherford showed that the central nucleus is very small and matter is therefore mostly empty space. There still remains much that we do not know about the makeup of matter.

1902. Mount Pelee is located on Martinique, a French island in the Caribbean region. A volcanic explosion occurred today, spreading a deadly cloud of hot gas across the island. In the city of Saint Pierre, 40,000 people perished almost instantly. Very few residents survived, one being a prisoner who was protected in a dungeon. This volcanic event shows the incredible heat energy which lies beneath our feet, deep underground.

1745. Yale, the third college established in the United States, today was chartered by Connecticut. Original rules at the school included the following:

— The president or a substitute shall pray in the college hall every morning and evening, and shall read a suitable portion of Scripture. Every absent undergraduate shall be fined one penny; those tardy shall pay a half penny.

— Any student guilty of blasphemy, fornication, robbery, or forgery shall be expelled.

— Any student who denies any part of Scripture or who tends to subvert the fundamentals of faith shall be expelled.

1869. The first transcontinental railroad was completed today when construction teams met at Promontory Summit, Utah. It took six years to lay the track between Sacramento, California, and Omaha, Nebraska. The final golden spike had engraved on its side, "May God continue the unity of our Country as the Railroad unites the two great Oceans of the World." The railroad leaders showed wisdom in stating that true unity comes only through recognition of the Creator.

MAY 10

The completion point for the first transcontinental railway.

1910. Glacier National Park in northwest Montana was established today by Congress. There are 50 active glaciers in the park and also many striking ice-sculptured rock formations. The area also includes the Lewis Overthrust, a large section of rock layers that are "out of place" in standard geology thinking. "Ancient" Precambrian rock is found to rest on top of much younger sedimentary beds. The usual explanation is that the older upper rock somehow slid horizontally for many miles, ending up at its present location. Creationists propose more simply that most of these rock layers formed in place, much as we find them, during the great flood of Noah's day.

1796. British physician Edward Jenner performed the first vaccination against disease this week. He inoculated a patient with a tiny amount of cowpox germs. The patient's body responded positively by building up a strong resistance to cowpox. This experiment demonstrated the body's amazing ability to produce antibodies and fight disease.

1903. A songbird thought to be extinct, Kirtland's Warbler, was rediscovered today. The few survivors nest in a tiny area of jack pines about 100 miles long and 60 miles wide located in north central Michigan. Kirtland's Warblers also migrate each fall and spend winter in the Bahamas. Today these rare birds are a federally protected endangered species. Instead of the natural evolutionary development of many new species, the task in recent years has been to maintain the species already created.

1948. Israel today was declared an independent country by the United Nations. Jewish survivors from World War II came together in Palestine to rebuild their nation. In the following decades Israel has become a strong, modern country. Many Christians see this regathering of Israel as a possible fulfillment of prophetic Scripture, as described in Jeremiah 29:14 and elsewhere.

MAY 14

MAY 15

1953. Stanley Miller published a famous paper in the journal *Science* today, titled "A Production of Amino Acids under Possible Primitive Earth Conditions." The University of Chicago experiment was an attempt to model conditions on the early earth and to duplicate the origin of life. Several gases were mixed with hot water vapor, then passed through a spark. The water represented the primordial ocean, and the spark provided an energy source similar to lightning. The experiment eventually produced simple amino acids. However, these results do not provide evidence for the spontaneous life generation on earth, for at least three reasons. *First*, oxygen was not used as one of the gases since it interferes with amino acid results. However, evidence shows that oxygen has always been present on earth. *Second*, the produced amino acids are a mixture of both right and left-handed molecules. However, almost all amino acids within living creatures are left-handed. *Third*, amino acids are at least 10,000 times simpler in content than the true building blocks of life such as proteins and cells. The scientific origin of life on earth remains an unsolved mystery. It appears that life always comes from life, ever since the moment of creation.

1956. An arctic tern was observed in Australia today, having migrated a record distance of 14,000 miles. The tern had been banded a year earlier in faraway Russia. There are reports of terns flying even farther, between Greenland and Australia. Another bird related to the arctic tern, the sooty tern, leaves its nesting grounds and spends 3–10 years continually in the air before returning to land. The common swift likewise remains airborne for 2–3 years. These amazing birds sleep, eat, and mate while in constant flight! Migration is a marvelous aspect of the creation. Scripture refers to the migration of the hawk (Job 39:26), and also the stork, dove, swift, and thrush (see Jer. 8:7).

1931. This week a letter in the journal *Nature* by Georges Lemaitre first proposed that the entire universe had begun from the expansion of a single, primordial atom. The Belgian priest and mathematician thus wrote the "original charter" of the big bang theory. This time was during the Great Depression and the U.S. news media widely promoted Lemaitre's idea in an attempt to create some scientific excitement and cheer. Lemaitre always insisted his theory had nothing to do with religion. In 1951 he disagreed when Pope Pius XII cited the big bang as evidence of creation. Many creationists would agree with Lemaitre that it is impossible to combine the big bang theory with the Genesis description of supernatural creation.

1901. The writer of the hymn *This Is My Father's World* died today in an accident. At the time Pastor Maltbie Babcock (1858–1901) was on a study trip to the Holyland. Babcock had a special love for students. He was in constant demand as a university campus preacher all across America. His well-known hymn reminds us that this is God's world, and the Creator is in complete control:

> This is my Father's world,
> And to my listening ears,
> All nature sings and round me rings
> The music of the spheres.

These spheres refer to the nine planets of the solar system. Like slowly vibrating violin strings, each planet orbits the sun with its own unique frequency. Furthermore, the planetary moons revolve, the stars rotate, and entire galaxies slowly turn. Since sound is defined as vibrations, perhaps the Lord and his angels truly enjoy the harmony of this celestial music.

• • • •

1980. Early on a Sunday morning, northwest America was shaken by a major eruption of Mount St. Helens in Washington state. The top 1,350 feet of the mountain cascaded into the Toutle River valley below, and dust clouds circled the earth for weeks to come. Since this time the location has provided a wonderful outdoor laboratory for study. The event has shown how quickly the geology of an area can change, including rapid formation of sedimentary layers, followed by catastrophic erosion. Just decades later, the Mount St. Helens region

Mount St. Helens erupts.

now illustrates the rapid recovery of trees, plants, and animals following such a catastrophe. Fish again swim in the rivers and lakes, and wildflowers bloom. The creation has a surprising ability to restore itself after large-scale alteration.

MAY
19

1910. There was great fear across the world today. The earth was about to pass directly through the tail of Halley's Comet. Dire stories circulated about poison cyanide gas that was present in the comet's tail. Many people

Halley's Comet.

sealed their windows with tape and also bought "comet pills" for their protection. When the passage actually occurred, however, there was no harm. The tenuous tail of a comet is a million miles long and is mostly empty space. On earth nothing could be seen, tasted, or smelled from the comet. The Creator did not make a solar system which endangers the life of mankind in this way. Instead, visible comets provide an enjoyable view of the faithful motions of the heavenly objects.

1875. The International Bureau of Weights and Measures was established today in France. There was a pressing need to standardize physical measurements in engineering, medicine, and other technical areas. Today it is realized that almost all physical quantities can be defined in terms of just three basic variables: length (feet, meters), mass (slugs, kilograms), and time (seconds). For example, speed is length divided by time, as in miles per hour.

MAY
20

There is something very fundamental about length, mass, and time in understanding the details of creation. All three quantities are also referred to indirectly in Genesis 1:1.

1965. Headlines in the *New York Times* today announced that the big bang theory at last had been proven true. Scientists Arno Penzias and Robert Wilson had detected a weak background radiation which permeates all of space. This invisible radiation has an energy equivalent to a temperature of -454°F (-270°C), just above absolute zero. The weak glow of radiation was interpreted as the "last dying ember" from the original super-hot big bang explosion of the universe billions of years earlier. However, the newspaper announcement was premature, since the big bang still remains an unproven theory today. If the creation was truly supernatural as Scripture declares, then it lies forever beyond scientific understanding.

1933. President Franklin D. Roosevelt proclaimed this date as National Maritime Day, a day on which coastal cities annually celebrate their sea heritage. Glouchester, Massachusetts, in particular, has long been a center for Atlantic fishing fleets. The statue of a sailor in Glouchester bears the words, "They that go down to the sea in ships. . . ." This is a portion of Psalm 107 which continues, "that do business in great waters; These see the works of the LORD" (Ps. 107:23–24). Sailors who travel the wide ocean certainly do come face to face with the power and majesty of the Creator.

MAY 23

1785. Benjamin Franklin today announced his invention of bifocal eyeglasses. Franklin studied all aspects of nature, from lenses to lightning. Bifocal optics also are found to occur in nature. A Caribbean fish, the *anableps*, is sometimes called the four-eyed fish because of its double retina. The top retina watches the sky above for enemy seabirds, while the bottom retina hunts for fish below. The Lord provided for all of His creatures in wonderful ways, including this unique fish. Every creature is complex and beyond our understanding.

MAY 24

1543. Polish astronomer Copernicus (1473–1543) died today. This same day his famous book *On the Revolutions of the Heavenly Spheres* was published. In the book Copernicus promoted the unpopular idea that the earth revolves about the sun. He had actually completed the book 13 years earlier, but the science authorities of his day did not allow the teaching of the heliocentric view. Our modern freedom to express personal views is a great privilege.

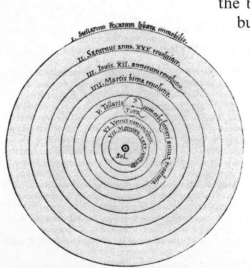

Coperniucus' solar model.

••••

1844. Today the first telegraph message was transmitted between Washington D.C. and Baltimore. Inventor Samuel Morse experimented for many years before this success. His very first transmitted sentence declared his honor for the Creator: "What hath God Wrought?" taken from Numbers 23:23. Just 22 years later, signals were being sent across the ocean by submerged telegraph cables (see July 27).

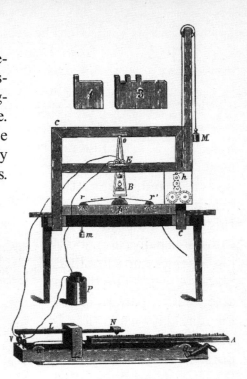

Morse telegraph.

MAY
25

1768. Today Captain James Cook set out on his first voyage of discovery to the South Pacific. For the next three years he explored many islands and also charted the coasts of New Zealand and West Australia. In this isolated part of the world, Cook found many native groups with mature cultures and governments. Clearly, people had rapidly spread across the earth following the Babel dispersion of Genesis 11. In many remote places they established ordered societies which still exist today.

MAY 26

1940. The evacuation of allied soldiers from Dunkirk, France, began today. Nearly 400,000 British, French, and Belgian troops were trapped on the French coastline during World War II. Nazi forces were just ten miles away, but could not attack because a thick fog had settled over the beaches. At this time the English Channel also became unusually calm, looking "as thick and smooth as black velvet." This favorable weather pattern lasted for nine days while the allied soldiers were transported safely to England. Winston Churchill called the evacuation of Dunkirk a "miracle of deliverance." The Creator indeed controls the details of history, including the weather.

Winston Churchill

MAY 27

1933. The World's Fair "Century of Progress" was opened today in Chicago in an unusual way. Light from the rising star Arcturus was captured by a telescope to activate switches and officially begin the celebration at the proper time. Why was Arcturus chosen? A previous World's Fair had been held in Chicago 40 years earlier, and Arcturus was known to be about 40 light years away. Therefore, as a promotional event, light that initially had left the star during the first fair was used to open the second fair. This story aptly demonstrates the immensity of space. Arcturus is a nearby star, today measured at 36 light years or about 200 trillion miles. Ever since 1933, Arcturus has been known as the World's Fair star.

MAY 28

585 B.C. Some have called this the first real date in history. Today a total solar eclipse occurred, just as predicted by the Greek philosopher Thales of Miletus. The temporary darkness so surprised citizens that an ongoing battle between the Medes and Lydians was called off. Total eclipses of the sun are rare and memorable events. Among all the planets and moons in the solar system, earth is the only location where perfect solar eclipses can occur. This is because the sun and moon are the same apparent size in the sky, so they can occasionally cover each other. The sun is actually about 400 times larger than the moon, but it is also 400 times farther away. Solar and lunar eclipses may well have been planned by the Creator to help us better understand the chronology of history.

MAY 29

1919. Today a solar eclipse provided an important test of Einstein's relativity prediction that starlight is slightly deflected by the sun's gravity. Sir Arthur Eddington led an expedition to the South Pacific to photograph the rare eclipse event. The successful results proved the correctness of Einstein's physics ideas. Had the experiment failed, Einstein stated that he would have been "sorry for the dear Lord [because] the theory is correct."

• • • •

1953. Today Sir Edmund Hillary and Tenzing Norkay became the first explorers to reach the summit of Mount Everest. Hillary was from New Zealand, and Norkay from Nepal. Their climb took 11 weeks with several bases set up along the way.

Mount Everest is a mountain of majestic extremes, with its peak standing 5.5 miles above sea level. It is located in the Himalaya Mountain range on the frontiers of Tibet and Nepal.

• • • •

1986. Today a biotechnology company in Wisconsin conducted initial trials of genetically engineered organisms. Foreign genes were inserted into tobacco plants to make them grow bigger. In following years biologists have sought to alter the offspring of many other plants and animals. This is a controversial research area, where science has progressed far ahead of ethical considerations. It may not please the Creator when mankind tampers with the created *kinds* of plants and animals.

MAY
30

1898. The element krypton was discovered today by scientists Alexander Ramsay and Morris Travers. Krypton occurs as a gas with no color, odor, or taste. It also forms very few chemical compounds. The name krypton means "hidden" in Greek. This year the same research team also identified the additional elements xenon and neon. Every element has its own unique properties and useful applications for mankind.

1889. Johnstown, Pennsylvania, was suddenly hit with a wall of water this afternoon when an earthen dam failed, following many days of heavy rains. This was one of the first great disasters in American history. The resulting destruction demonstrated the awesome force of raging floodwaters.  Large trees were uprooted, and 34 train engines were lifted from railroad tracks. The lives lost totaled 2,200. This local flood gives a brief glimpse of the magnitude of the far greater flood of Noah's day.

 1845. A distance record was set by a homing pigeon today. The ambitious traveler completed a 6,600-mile (11,000 km) journey between Namibia, Africa and its home base in London. The 55-day trip had crossed both desert and sea. The precise homing instinct of these small creatures defies our understanding. Somehow their senses return them unfailingly to their place of origin, no matter how far away. Bird flight and navigation are wonders of creation (see May 16).

1966. The American space probe *Surveyor 1* reached the moon's surface today. The goal was to determine whether a manned landing was possible. Some scientists had predicted a dangerously thick layer of lunar dust. *Surveyor* made the first lunar soft landing in a smooth region called Oceanus Procellarium. Pictures showed only a thin covering of dust. The Apollo program of manned lunar exploration followed during the next few years, with 12 astronauts eventually walking on the moon.

JUNE 3

1726. This is the birthdate of Scottish geologist James Hutton (1726–1797). His 1785 book *Theory of the Earth* profoundly shaped modern geology. Hutton believed that "the present is the key to the past." That is, slow, gradual changes have shaped the earth. He wrote that he saw "no vestige of a beginning, no prospect of an end" for the earth. This belief in slow changes over geologic time is today called the Principle of Uniformitarianism or Gradualism. It misinterprets earth history by not acknowledging unique past events such as the creation of a fully functioning earth and also the Genesis flood event. The belief in gradual, slow changes over an immense time span greatly influenced geologist Charles Lyell and also Charles Darwin.

• • • •

1769. A famous transit of Venus across the face of the sun occurred today. On such rare occasions there is a direct lineup between the earth, Venus, and the sun. Venus then appears as a small black dot gliding across the solar disk for a duration of several minutes. Venus transits occur in pairs, about eight years apart, once a century. Captain James Cook traveled to Tahiti to observe this particular rare event during the first of his great voyages of discovery to the South Pacific. Cook's measurements of Venus helped determine the earth's exact distance from the sun. Transits show the dependability of the laws that have been established to maintain the stability of the physical creation.

1844. The last of the Great Auks, a penguin-like bird, was killed today. Auks were once plentiful in Greenland and Iceland. Many had died when an island near Iceland disappeared during an 1830 earthquake. Others were hunted to extinction for food and also for use as museum displays. Instead of observing the rapid evolution of new creatures, we instead see the loss of the created kinds due to many factors.

JUNE
4

JUNE
5

1940. The first auto tire made of synthetic rubber was exhibited today in Akron, Ohio. Over the years great effort has been made to artificially duplicate natural rubber. Over a million tons of natural rubber are still harvested each year worldwide. Rubber trees are grown on plantations in many tropical countries. Natural latex is collected from the trees and treated in various ways to produce the particular kind of rubber desired. Renewable resources such as rubber are an important gift to mankind.

1936. A breakthrough in the refining of petroleum occurred today. A research refinery in New Jersey produced aviation gasoline for the first time. Natural petroleum from the ground is a complex mixture of hydrocarbons, originating largely from buried vegetation. Much of it surely resulted from the Genesis flood event, when vast quantities of biomass were buried in sedimentary rock layers. The following list gives a few of the

JUNE
6

products derived from the refining of oil, along with their applications:

> petroleum ether (solvent)
> aviation fuel
> gasoline
> kerosene (fuel, lighting)
> lubricating oil
> paraffin (candles, waxed paper)
> asphalt (paving, roofing)
> coke (fuel)

JUNE 7

1946. An early computer began operating this month. It was called Eniac, short for "Electronic numerical integrator and computer." This computer contained 18,000 vacuum tubes, weighed 30 tons, and filled a large room. Today's small personal computers have a far greater capacity than Eniac. Progress in computer design with solid state electronics has occurred steadily over the decades. However, all computers remain far less complex than that provided for each of us within our heads. The human brain is the most advanced computer ever known.

1940. Researchers today made the new element neptunium by bombarding uranium atoms with neutrons. This radioactive element also occurs in nature in small amounts. Neptunium has a complex nucleus filled with 93 protons and 144 or more neutrons. The

JUNE 8

heavier elements of the periodic table such as neptunium are less familiar than the lighter elements. However, they greatly help our understanding of chemistry and the creation in general.

JUNE 9

1959. A nuclear submarine was launched today from the shipyard at Groton, Connecticut. The *George Washington* was the first submarine to carry missiles for American defense. It was 380 feet long and weighed over 5,000 tons. Modern submarines are modeled somewhat after the shape of whales. Many whales, like the sperm and blue whales, were designed by their maker with blunt heads. This shape has been found to help them glide through water with the least effort. Since submarines travel at speeds similar to whales, these vessels also are designed with blunt bows. There is much practical information to be found in nature. This should be no surprise because the Master Designer made all things.

JUNE 10

1955. The first separation of a virus into its component parts was announced today. German biochemist H. Fraenkel-Conrat in Berkeley, California, showed that viruses consist of a protein coating and a nucleic-acid interior. Viruses can invade host cells and then reprogram the cells to help the virus reproduce itself. About 100 different viruses are known to cause human disease. Such activity surely relates to the curse of Genesis 3, when sin first cast its shadow of suffering over the creation.

1770. The Great Barrier Reef along Australia's east coast was discovered today by accident. During the night, Captain James Cook ran his British ship *Endeavour* onto the reef causing minor damage. This reef is possibly the largest living entity on earth. It runs for a thousand miles offshore and consists of billions of tiny host creatures called polyps. Colorful sea creatures make the Great Barrier Reef a wonderful area for scuba diving and snorkeling. The variety and color of undersea creatures are unmatched anywhere else on earth.

1979. An amazing flight across the English Channel occurred today. Cyclist Bryan Allen successfully pedaled a mechanical plane called the *Gossamer Albatross* just above the waves, from England to France, about 25 miles. Great effort continues to improve man-powered

flight. At the creation, God gave many creatures the ability to fly, including birds; insects; mammals, such as bats; and certain reptiles. Our efforts continue to duplicate their flight.

1938. Chlorophyll is the green pigment in plants which absorbs light energy. Carbon dioxide and water are then converted to carbohydrate and oxygen by way of photosynthesis. This week the artificial synthesis of chlorophyll was patented by Benjamin Grushkin. A material that occurs commonly in nature was thus patented for the first time by a scientist. Chlorophyll is a very complex material, and its conversion of sunlight to chemical energy is poorly understood. All forms of created life depend on chlorophyll for their survival.

• • • •

1824. The only book written by scientist Sadi Carnot (1796–1832) was published this week, titled *Reflections on the Native Power of Fire*. Carnot brilliantly described two basic laws of energy. First, energy cannot be created or destroyed, and second, useful energy becomes unavailable over time. Carnot was a pioneer in studying these rules of nature, now called the first and second laws of thermodynamics. They are the most basic findings in all of science. They declare that the universe was created with dependable rules. Carnot was far ahead of his time, and his book was unrecognized and largely forgotten for 25 years. Carnot unfortunately died at the young age of 36 during a cholera epidemic in France.

1954. Today an important addition was made to America's *Pledge of Allegiance*. A shortened pledge had been first published in 1892 in Boston. Today President Eisenhower signed an order adding the words "under God" to the pledge:

JUNE
14

> I pledge allegiance to the flag of the United States of America and to the republic for which it stands, one nation *under God*, indivisible, with liberty and justice for all.

All U.S. citizens benefit from the godly heritage of their country.

1752. Benjamin Franklin performed his famous kite experiment today during a thunderstorm. He stood with his son under cover from the rain on the outskirts of Philadelphia. Fortunately they were not injured by lightning. Franklin's understanding of the electrical nature of lightning soon led to his invention of lightning rods. The next year he wrote in his *Poor Richard's Almanac*, "It has pleased God in his goodness to mankind, at length [to reveal] to them the means of securing their habitations and other buildings from mischief by thunder and lightning." Lightning is necessary in providing nitrogen for the earth's soil. With lightning rods, the Creator also provides an effective safety mechanism for this natural hazard.

Benjamin Franklin experiments with lightning and a kite.

1980. In a landmark decision, the U.S. Supreme Court ruled today that new organisms made in the laboratory could be patented. What is commonly done is to alter genetic material in an existing organism. The technique has  been employed, for example, to make bacteria that synthesize insulin and other human proteins. The government ruling remains controversial. Many people feel that any benefits derived from genetic engineering belong equally to all people, and should not be subject to patent protection (see May 29).

1963. The Supreme Court today ruled that local and state laws requiring the recitation of Scripture or the Lord's Prayer in public schools were unconstitutional. Vigorous opponents of prayer have largely succeeded in removing all visible symbols of Christianity from classrooms. In this way students have been robbed of an understanding of the biblical heritage of America. Christian teachers face special challenges in today's public classrooms. Thankfully, private school and home school options are also available.

1178. Monks in Canterbury, England, reported a strange sight tonight. While gazing upward they noticed the distant flash of a large explosion that apparently came from the far side of the moon.

Today there remains a large crater where

an object, perhaps an asteroid, collided with the lunar surface. It is called Crater Giordano Bruno and is 20 miles (32 km) in diameter. This is the only observation ever recorded of a major lunar collision.

JUNE 19

240 B.C. Records show this to be the possible week of an important ancient measurement. Actually the day and year are not precisely known. Eratosthenes was a Greek astronomer interested in the curvature of the earth. By noting the length of shadows, he was able to calculate the earth's circumference. Eratosthenes came surprisingly close to the actual value, which is about 24,870 miles. Ancient Greek scientists therefore not only realized the earth was round, but they also knew its size. Through the ages God has given people the ability to study and understand the world He made.

1782. Colonial Americans this week chose the bald eagle as their national emblem. Benjamin Franklin was unhappy with the choice, preferring the turkey! The majestic eagle today lives only in North America and Siberia. It likes to perch in high places along rivers and lakes. From such heights eagles are able to see targets just one foot in size at a distance of two miles. Eagles have a visual resolving power 50–100 times greater than the human eye. Every animal on earth displays created complexity. Bald eagles are now protected from hunting in all states.

JUNE 20

The summer solstice occurs each year around June 21–23. At this time the sun is at its maximum position north of the equator. In the Northern Hemisphere daylight is longest and nights are shortest around this date. The summer solstice marks the beginning of summer in the north, and winter in the Southern Hemisphere. According to Genesis 8:22, the repeating seasons show God's faithfulness.

1978. Charon, the only known moon of planet Pluto, was discovered tonight at the U.S. Naval Observatory in Washington, D.C. This unusual natural satellite is one-half the size of Pluto and orbits the planet in only about six days. Our own moon circles the earth once each month. The unexpected variety of solar system objects continues to baffle natural origin theories.

1925. Heavy rains fell this week in the Gros Ventre Mountains of Wyoming. Water seeping into the ground had dangerously loosened underground rock layers on the mountainsides. Suddenly a great rockslide occurred into the valley below. The Gros Ventre River was completely dammed, forming a new 3-mile-long lake. A short time later this natural dam broke and water rushed through the valley town of Kelly, killing many citizens. Raging water, when unleashed, causes great destruction. Such disasters are a reminder of the judgment by water during the Genesis flood.

• • • •

1998. A press conference was held today at the National Geographic Society. It concerned the discovery of two "feathered dinosaur" fossils in China. The conclusion was that modern birds must have long ago evolved from small dinosaurs. This conclusion is faulty on at least two counts. *First*, the prints in stone show fully functional feathers, not a structure somewhere between scales and feathers. *Second*, modern bird fossils are found in rocks which formed much earlier (see September 30). The Chinese discovery was likely a flightless bird, somewhat similar to the ostrich.

1878. An article appeared in this week's journal *Nature* concerning the speed of light. Albert Michelson had succeeded in measuring light speed with great accuracy. At this time he was only 26 years old and was an instructor at the U.S. Naval Academy. Light travels at 186,000 miles per second, the "speed limit" of the universe. Only prayers travel faster than light!

JUNE
24

JUNE
25

1950. This spring the English astronomer Fred Hoyle gave a series of radio talks for the British Broadcasting Corporation on "The Nature of the Universe." The actual date is uncertain, but during one program Hoyle originated the term *big bang*. While discussing origin theories, Hoyle said:

Broadly speaking, the older ideas fall into two groups. One was that the Universe started its life a finite time ago in a single huge explosion and that the present expansion is a relic of the violence of this explosion. This *big bang* idea seemed to me to be unsatisfactory even before detailed examination showed that it leads to serious difficulties.

A half-century later, many still agree with Fred Hoyle's sentiments regarding weaknesses of the big bang theory.

1974. Bar codes were first used today at a supermarket checkout in Ohio. These patterns of dark lines contain detailed information about the product, coded into binary numbers. Bar codes now appear on most letters, books, and general merchandise. These binary codes are part of the worldwide "information revolution." Much planning goes into the design and reading of these codes. On a deeper level, all living things carry complex DNA codes which fully describe the organism. Just as bar codes require a designer, so does all life existing on earth.

1969. An article in today's *Science* periodical described a new material called polywater. Russian chemists claimed to have prepared this strange new form of water which boiled at 1,000°F and froze at -40°F. Polywater also did not evaporate, and it resembled a clear syrupy substance. Some scientists feared that polywater might pose a threat to life on earth. If released, the polywater might quickly trigger a conversion of all the earth's natural water to the unusual new form. If this happened, normal liquid water then would no longer be available anywhere. There would be no rain, humidity, or drinking water. Additional studies soon showed that polywater actually did not exist. The original Russian samples contained normal water which was contaminated with other chemicals. The Creator did not make this world with bizarre materials that threaten to extinguish life. Instead, normal water is provided for us as an essential ingredient for life.

1820. The tomato, thought to be poisonous, today was shown to be edible in a public demonstration in Europe. For a long time the tomato had been grown as an ornamental plant. However, the red fruit was regarded with suspicion because the plant itself is similar to deadly nightshade. Tomato roots and leaves do indeed contain poisons, but the fruit is healthy and loaded with vitamin C. Tomatoes are a wonderful food source created for our benefit.

JUNE
28

• • • •

1983. The Glen Canyon Dam controls the Colorado River just above the Grand Canyon. This dam forms Lake Powell in Arizona and Utah. During 1983 the lake was flooded by excessive snowmelt. On this date engineers were forced to open a 40-foot-diameter spillway to prevent the high water from overflowing the dam. As 32,000 cubic feet of water per second rushed through the manmade tunnel, the ground rumbled and vibrated. The force of the water soon eroded completely through the steel-reinforced concrete lining of the tunnel. Large chunks of concrete and pulverized rock were hurled outward with the water into the river below. The water tunnel quickly was closed and then repaired with

63,000 cubic feet of new concrete lining. This episode of near-failure of the Glen Canyon Dam demonstrates the power of moving water to rapidly erode the earth beyond all predictions.

JUNE 29

1906. Today Mesa Verde National Park was established in southwest Colorado. This site of ancient cliff dwellings reveals a rich Indian culture that flourished as long as 2,000 years ago. Cliff Palace, built under a great sandstone ledge, is a complex of over 200 rooms where 250 people once lived. Jewelry and trading materials reveal the artistic ability of these Indians of the Southwest. The park shows that early Americans were by no means a primitive people. And even as early as Genesis 4:21–22 there is mention of individuals skilled in music and metallurgy. The primitive, ape-man picture of our early ancestors is clearly wrong.

1860. A famous debate on origins occurred today at the British Association for the Advancement of Science. Samuel Wilberforce challenged evolutionist Thomas Huxley with a question: "I would like to ask the gentlemen . . . whether the ape from which he descended was on his grandmother's or his grandfather's side of the family."

JUNE 30

Huxley replied that he would rather be related to an ape than to a person like Wilberforce! Clearly, both spokesmen were provoking each other. More recent debates on this origins issue have succeeded in showing the solid scientific evidence for creation.

1908. This morning the earth was struck by a large space object. Passengers on the Trans-Siberian Railroad watched a bright light race across the sky, followed by thunder and a blast of hot air. In the Tunguska River region of Siberia there resulted a large, shallow crater that has since become a frozen lake. Trees were flattened for 20 miles in all directions. It appears that the object, a large meteorite or comet, may have exploded several miles above the ground. Some worry about a similar comet collision with a large city. On a biblical time scale, however, the chance of such an event is negligible. The historical collisions that the earth *has* experienced have generally occurred in remote areas like Siberia or the sea.

JULY 1

1993. Today a drill penetrated through the thickest part of Greenland's ice sheet, 1.8 miles deep. A hollow drill was used which preserved a 4-inch cylindrical core of ice for later study. Such ice cores provide detailed information on the past climate. One surprising result is how quickly the climate warmed at the end of the Ice Age, just a few thousand years ago. Earth's average temperatures increased by 6° C within just a few years' time. Many creationists believe that this Ice Age followed the Genesis flood. Other studies have shown that Greenland truly was once green. The preflood world was entirely warm and tropical in climate.

1566. Nostradamus (1503–1566) was a French physician and astrologer who became very popular as one who could predict the future. This is the day Nostradamus died, a date which he had

JULY 2

predicted ahead of time. His prophecies include the deaths of popes, future world wars, and even the end of the world. Nostradamus wrote very obscurely, and in a mixture of several languages. He claimed to have received some of his mystical ideas from wave patterns observed while stirring a bucket of water! How much more certain and clear are the prophecies given to us by

Nostradamus

the Creator in Scripture. Nostradamus' prediction of his death today was not unusual. At the time he was suffering from several severe afflictions of his day, including gout and dropsy.

1948. This week the first transistor was demonstrated by researchers at Bell Telephone Laboratories. This small solid-state device performs the function of much larger vacuum tubes, and with greatly reduced power needs. Transistors helped begin the modern electronics revolution which continues today. Semi-conducting materials such as germanium and silicon, long thought to be worthless, now reveal the practical potential created within them.

JULY 3

The first "transfer resistor" or transistor, demonstrated by scientists from Bell Laboratories on Christmas Eve 1947, was a couple of inches wide.

A.D. 1054. It is appropriate that this traditional day of fireworks in the United States also marks the observation of a famous supernova or exploding star. Such a star flared brightly in the night sky tonight and was recorded by Chinese and Arab astronomers. The starlight slowly faded over the next year, leaving behind a cloud of gas debris. This still-expanding cloud is today called the Crab Nebula, visible in December skies to telescopes. As Scripture declares, the heavens are slowly wearing out, including the stars themselves.

HST

Palomar

Crab Nebula
Hubble Space Telescope · Wide Field Planetary Camera 2

PRC96-22a · ST ScI OPO · May 30, 1996 · J. Hester and P. Scowen (AZ State Univ.) and NASA

• • • •

1776. "We hold these Truths to be self-evident, that all Men are created equal, that they are endowed by their Creator with certain unalienable Rights, that among these are Life, Liberty and the Pursuit of Happiness." So begins the second paragraph of the Declaration of Independence, acknowledging the Creator of the universe. The famous document was adopted by the Continental Congress in Philadelphia on this birthday of the United States.

1687. Isaac Newton's *Principia* was published on this date. His classic book laid the foundation for our present understanding of astronomy, physics, and calculus. Newton's friend Edmund Halley assisted in financing the printing of the book. As the purpose for writing this famous book Newton wrote, "I had an eye upon such Principles as might work with considering men for belief in a Deity." Isaac Newton firmly believed in the Creator of the universe.

1885. Today physician Louis Pasteur treated a patient who had been bitten by a rabid dog. Pasteur injected a rabies vaccine that he earlier had prepared from rabbits; the patient then quickly recovered his health. This successful inoculation showed the body's

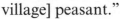

amazing ability to make antibodies to fight disease. Pasteur remained a Christian all his life. When asked how he related the Bible and science knowledge, he said, "The more I know, the more does my faith approach that of the Breton [a French village] peasant."

1955. The whooping crane is named for its loud, bugle-like call. Once common in the United States, their numbers dwindled greatly a century ago. By 1937

only 15 known cranes remained alive. They wintered in Texas marshes but no one knew where their eggs were laid each spring. On this particular date the whooping cranes were found nesting in northern Alberta, Canada. They had moved far north from their original breeding grounds in the Great Plains states. Now carefully monitored and protected, there are more than 100 whooping cranes alive today. It is the tallest American bird at five feet, and one of the rarest in the world.

1978. Today the Italian climber Reinhold Messner reached the summit of Mount Everest without carrying extra oxygen. At this altitude of over 29,000 feet, the lack of atmospheric oxygen quickly drains one's energy. Messner has gone on since then to climb 14 of the world's highest peaks, all without oxygen. The earth's beneficial atmosphere is a mixture of mainly nitrogen, oxygen, carbon dioxide, and argon gases. Gravity keeps this precious air from escaping the earth completely and extinguishing life.

JULY 8

JULY 9

1893. The first successful heart surgery took place today in Chicago. A patient's artery had been damaged by a knife wound. Surgeon Daniel Williams stitched the wound and the fortunate patient recovered. This operation was later described in the journal *Medical Record*. Each human heart is a marvel of design. This tireless organ pumps blood throughout the body and beats normally about 70 times per minute by coordinated nerve impulses and muscular contraction. During an average life-time the heart beats more than 2.5 billion times.

1962. The first active communication satellite, *Telstar I*, was launched today from Florida. It successfully began re-laying trans-Atlantic television pic-tures. Years later, we take for granted our worldwide televised news coverage. Hundreds of satellites now circle the earth, tethered by the earth's invisible gravity. Satellites are useful for research, photography, weather prediction, military se-curity, and communication.

1828. French scientist Jean Baptiste Lamarck (1744–1829) believed that plants and animals evolved by inherit-ing acquired characteristics. For ex-ample, he suggested that giraffes gradu-ally grew longer necks by stretching to reach leaves in treetops. Lamarck assumed that "vital fluids" flowed to a giraffe's neck, somehow caus-ing extra growth. The idea was ridiculed even during Lamarck's lifetime. This particular calendar date marks the forced departure of Lamarck from the French Academy of Science. For the remaining 18 months of his life he remained alone and silent. This was a sad conclusion to a science ca-reer which had excluded the Creator. Lamarck's own words:

Neither man nor anything else in the world is the result of special creation. That belief is childish, fit only for primitive people.

Two centuries later, the creation movement thrives while Lamarck's evolutionary ideas are rejected.

1964. Bids were opened today for an ambitious geology project. Project Mohole was a plan to drill more than ten miles deep directly through the earth's crust and into the mantle beneath. Six years and $10 million later, the U.S. government project was finally abandoned due to technical difficulties. The extreme heat and pressure of the lower crust simply made deep drilling impossible. The earth's mantle was not yet ready to reveal its secrets. The deepest hole drilled since then was in northern Russia, 7.5 miles deep. These holes are only a fraction of the crustal thickness. One is reminded of Jeremiah 31:37:

JULY
12

> If heaven above can be measured, and the foundations of the earth searched out beneath, I will also cast off all the seed of Israel for all that they have done, saith the LORD (KJV).

This verse places a basic limit on our scientific understanding of the depths of the earth as well as the high heavens. Indeed, we have very limited knowledge either of the earth's interior or of deep space.

JULY
13

1869. Diamonds were discovered today in a farm field near present-day Kimberley in South Africa. The resulting Kimberley mine soon became the richest diamond producer in the world. In South Africa, diamonds are commonly found within "diamond pipes" composed of the mineral kimberlite. Geologists assume that the diamonds form about 75 miles deep in the earth under high pressure, then are carried to the surface by the upward kimberlite while in a molten state. In early history gold and gemstones were found near the Garden of Eden (Gen. 2:12). Precious stones including diamond were part of the breastplate worn by the high priest at the time of Moses (Exod. 28:15–21). Thus, it is likely that surface diamonds also were part of the original creation.

1989. The world's most powerful particle accelerator began operation today. This "atom smasher" or collider was built by CERN, the Europeon Center for Nuclear Research. Located in Geneva, Switzerland, the machine has probed details of the smallest particles known, called quarks. It is also CERN which helped begin the Internet, originally designed to tie its own laboratory computers together. Today the Internet connects millions of computers all around the world. No matter how sophisticated the Internet becomes, however, the Creator's communication link is still greater. He hears all our prayers at once, and is not subject to power failure or computer error.

1662. The Royal Society of London was chartered today. This science society began "for the improving of natural knowledge" and "its members should be directed to the glory of God." One of the founders was Robert Boyle, known as the father of chemistry and also a strong Christian. The much-respected Royal Society has been home to many outstanding creation scientists such as Isaac Newton, Michael Faraday, and Lord Kelvin. The society continues today, although far removed from its religious roots.

JULY 16

1945. Early this morning the Alamogordo, New Mexico, desert was suddenly lit up by the first atomic explosion. Years of scientific study and preparation by the United States resulted in this frightening energy display, a million times greater than any conventional explosion. The Creator has placed untold amounts of energy within the nuclei of atoms. Unfortunately, this resource has often been limited to military weapons instead of being used for exploring the creation and producing useful energy.

The world's first explosion of an atomic bomb.

1959. Today Louis and Mary Leakey discovered *Zinjanthropus* or "East-African Man" at the Olduvai Gorge in Tanzania, East Africa. This fossil has been strongly promoted as our human ancestor. Actually, it is placed in the Australopithecine category and is 100 per-

cent animal. An unquestioned direct link between people and animals has never been found. This is not surprising since the Book of Genesis clearly states that mankind has a distinct origin from the animal world.

1691. Robert Boyle wrote out his will today, just six months before his death at age 64. He had spent a productive career in science, and often is called the father of modern chemistry. Boyle was distinguished by his genius, virtues, and benevolence. A strong Christian, Boyle supported many missionaries and also financed the translation of Scripture into Irish and Turkish languages. His will established the Boyle Lectures, annual presentations in support of creation and Christianity. In Boyle's own words, the lectures are "for proving the Christian religion against notorious infidels." These lectures continue today in England, but on secular scientific subjects.

1994. Twenty comet fragments slammed into the planet Jupiter during this week. The multiple collisions from Comet Shoemaker-Levy led to tremendous explosions on Jupiter which were observed with telescopes. Each impact

released energy equivalent to trillions of tons of TNT. The large outer planets actually protect the earth from such a catastrophe. Their gravity attracts space debris that might otherwise hit the earth. The created earth enjoys a peaceful existence as an inner planet in the midst of the occasional violence of space.

JULY 20

1969. After a three-day, 239,000 mile trip, the *Apollo 11* space mission finally reached earth's nearest neighbor, the moon. The Eagle lander settled onto the lunar surface today and Neil Armstrong became the first man to take

One small step for [a] man, one giant leap for mankind.

President Richard Nixon called this the "greatest week in the history of the world since the creation." Study of the moon has not resulted in a convincing natural lunar origin theory as originally hoped for. Instead, the moon remains a strong testimony to a miraculous beginning on the fourth day of creation week, by God's word.

JULY 21

1820. Danish scientist Hans Christian Oersted (1777–1851) wrote an important paper today. It summarized a discovery he had just made while giving a school lecture. Producing an electric current in a wire, he noticed the deflection of a nearby compass needle. This needle movement showed that electricity and magnetism are closely related by an invisible force. From this simple beginning came the entire field of electrodynamics with the invention of generators and motors. Oersted wrote that he was motivated by the belief that "all phenomena are produced by the same original power," a direct reference to the Creator. He also wrote that he clearly saw the hand of God in the beauty and unity of nature. Many pioneers of science and technology likewise believed firmly in creation.

JULY 22

1925. During the Scopes trial this week, creationist William Jennings Bryan made many memorable statements including these:

> When I read [in the Bible] that a big fish swallowed Jonah — it does not say whale — I believe it. And I believe in a God who can make a whale and can make a man and make both do what He pleases.

> I believe in the Rock of Ages, not the age of Rocks.

Actually, the creation position does not oppose the scientific study of whales, rocks, or stars. Science, correctly handled, is not an enemy of creation. Valid scientific study and data interpretation bring us closer to the Creator and his works.

JULY 23

1937. One of the hormones produced by the pituitary gland was isolated today at the Yale School of Medicine in Connecticut. Until this time the pituitary gland was considered a useless, vestigial organ from our evolutionary past. The pituitary gland is located at the base of the brain and serves several vital functions. Its hormones control growth, regulate the thyroid gland, and also direct metabolic processes. Many decades after the Yale hormone study, the complexity of the pituitary gland still defies human understanding. It is not a vestigial organ, but instead is a direct evidence for creation.

JULY 24

1925. Today John T. Scopes was found guilty of teaching evolution in a Dayton, Tennessee, high school. The trial ran for 15 days and Scopes was fined a token $100. Creationist William Jennings Bryan debated evolutionist Clarence Darrow during this famous "monkey" trial. Many attenders were caught up in the circus-like atmosphere, not realizing the serious assault taking place on biblical values. The popular play *Inherit the Wind* is a misleading account of the event (see April 21).

JULY 25

1976. Today the *Viking I* space probe analyzed Martian soil for signs of life. The instrument had landed on Mars four days earlier. At a cost of $60 million this message was transmitted back to earth: There is no sign of life whatsoever on Mars. Evidently the Creator did not choose to place life on Mars, and it certainly did not begin there on its own (see August 7).

JULY 26

1963. The first synchronous satellite was placed in orbit today. These special satellites circle the earth at an altitude of 22,300 miles. At this distance they orbit the earth in exactly 24 hours and therefore appear to hang motionless at a given point above the earth's equator. Actually the synchronous satellites travel at about 7,000 miles per hour, faster than a bullet. Such satellites are very useful for communication, research, and weather study.

1866. Today an undersea telegraph cable successfully connected America and Europe for the first time, after years of attempts. The steamship *Great Eastern* succeeded in laying the cable beneath the Atlantic Ocean. Great effort has been made over the years to improve communication worldwide. In contrast, prayer requires no such temporary cable, and provides direct, unfailing access to the Creator.

JULY 27

JULY 28

1868. Today the Fourteenth Amendment to the U.S. Constitution was ratified. Directly following the Civil War, this amendment guaranteed the newly freed slaves their full rights as citizens. Slavery was tolerated in biblical times but was neither condoned nor promoted in Scripture. The creation view regards all people as equal in God's sight. One person should not own another.

1588. Today the English soundly de-
feated the Spanish Armada in the
Battle of Gravelines. Philip II of
Spain earlier had set out to conquer
England and Holland. His goal was
to unite all of Europe under the Catholic faith and with Spanish control. He

boasted of his "invincible" armada of 130 warships and
30,000 men.

However, bad weather struck his fleet off England's
coast. With no safe port available the Spanish ships were
forced to anchor at sea. A small British fleet under the command of Sir Francis Drake then harassed the Spanish by
releasing flaming "tar ships" among the anchored fleet. The
armada cut their anchors loose and fled north around Scot-
land where many ships were wrecked on the rocky shores.
As the older history books say, "God blew and they were
scattered."

Only half the original Spanish fleet survived to limp
back home again. Spain's great sea power had been broken
by the weather instead of by war. Perhaps a worldwide dic-
tatorship was averted by the Creator's providential use of
the wind.

1921. Scientists today announced that
laboratory-produced insulin was a successful treatment for diabetes. This discovery has given health and hope to
millions of people with diabetes. Insulin is a hormone normally made by the
pancreas. The essential chemical insulin acts
to regulate the level of glucose in our blood. The normal
chemical balance within the human body is a marvel of engineering design.

1990. The first gene therapy for patients was approved today by U.S. officials. The treatment was for a particular genetic disease which destroys the immune system. In the coming decades, genetic medicine will be greatly expanded to relieve suffering. Gene therapy shows great potential for improving human health. Ongoing research reveals the truth of David's words long ago:

JULY
31

> I praise you because I am fearfully and wonderfully made; your works are wonderful, I know that full well (Ps. 139:14).

AUGUST
1

1839. An accident occurred sometime this week, changing the career of Matthew Maury. He was a U.S. naval officer with dreams of sailing around the world. However, a stagecoach accident in Ohio severely injured his leg at the age of 33. Confined at home, he turned his interest to the study of ocean currents. Maury gathered data from thousands of ship logs to determine worldwide ocean current patterns. Maury later said he was motivated by Psalm 8:8 which describes the "paths of the seas." His mapping of these invisible paths of current has been of great value to sea travel ever since. Maury was later honored with the title "Pathfinder of the Seas," inscribed on his tombstone at the U.S. Naval Academy in Maryland.

AUGUST
2

1841. The term *dinosaur* was first coined today by Richard Owen, an English paleontologist. This is one of several possible dates cited for his "Report on British Fossil Reptiles." It was presented at a science conference during which he spoke for two and one-half hours! Owen chose the name dinosaur to establish a distinct title for these impressive creatures. The Greek *dinos* means "terrible" or "fearfully great"; *saur* means "lizard." This name was chosen to engender awe and respect for these impressive creatures. During the talk Owen declared that dinosaurs had not evolved from a lower order but had been directly created by God. Concerning limited variation within animal kinds, Owen believed that the "Divine mind which planned the Archetype also foreknew all its modifications."

AUGUST 3

1492. Christopher Columbus set sail today from Spain with 88 crewmen aboard three small ships called the *Nina, Pinta,* and *Santa Maria.* Columbus believed that his voyage was divinely directed as part of God's purpose for the world. His name means "Christbearer." Columbus wrote that God "granted me the gift of knowledge . . . [and] revealed to me that it was feasible to sail . . . to the Indies." He was also very interested in biblical history. Among his preserved papers is a chart entitled "An account of the Creation of the world according to the Jews." It recounts the years from Adam up through A.D. 1481. Christopher Columbus clearly accepted the literal creation account of Genesis (see October 12).

• • • •

1769. Today an amazing discovery was made by an explorer in present-day Los Angeles. Gaspar de Portola found a large pool of asphalt with entrapped animal remains, now called the La Brea Tar Pits. Scientists have excavated over ten thousand animal fossils from the mire, including saber-toothed tigers, llamas, giant wolves, and horses. The animals apparently wandered into the pool and became trapped. In addition, there are abundant insects, mollusks, and microscopic plants. Many of the animals show signs of having died during a stressful time of geologic upheaval and possible flooding. This may have occurred during the centuries following the great flood of Noah's day.

1958. The submarine U.S.S. *Nautilus* made history this week. During August 1–5 it completed a cruise completely beneath the thick ice cap at the North Pole. As the first nuclear-powered submarine, the *Nautilus* was able to remain submerged for long periods of time. Unlike the North Pole, Antarctica in the far south has thick ice lying on a foundation of rock. Most of the earth's fresh water supply exists as ice in these polar regions.

1782. Today William Paley (1743–1805) was appointed "Archdeacon of Carlisle" in the Church of England. He had come a long way from his youthful years of rebellion and lethargy. Now a preacher and writer, Paley strongly defended Scripture. His *Natural Theology* was published in 1802. This book opens with the well-known story of a person who finds a watch lying upon a path. It is obvious that someone made this intricate watch. It is likewise obvious that the complex world itself requires a designer or watchmaker. Whether one considers a snowflake or the human eye, the earth is filled with God's handiwork.

Design may be the best known argument for the existence of God. For many people it continues to be persuasive and convicting. Romans 1:20 remarks that the visible objects in creation are a sufficient evidence of God's existence.

1954. In this month's *Scientific American* biologist George Wald (1906–1997) wrote an article on evolution theory. In it he tried to explain how life began long ago on earth:

AUGUST
6

> Given so much time, the "impossible" becomes possible, the possible probable, and the probable virtually certain. One has only to wait: time itself performs the miracles.

Wald was a Harvard professor and Nobel Prize winner. In this quote he declares his faith in an immense geologic time scale which somehow makes the spontaneous origin of life inevitable. In truth, decades after Wald's article, scientists are no closer to solving the mystery of the origin of life on earth. The creation view declares that the origin of life is miraculous, and therefore entirely beyond the realm of our limited scientific understanding. God is the miracle worker, not time alone.

AUGUST
7

1996. During a dramatic press conference today, scientists announced the possible discovery of life on Mars. A meteorite found in Antarctica ten years earlier was thought to have originated on Mars. This rock showed signs of organic material and microscopic tube-shaped formations, possible signs of life. Later, most scientists rejected the fossil interpretation and believe the features are nonliving crystal material.

If there is any life in space, then either God placed it there or it may have been swept outward from the earth. The probability of the spontaneous origin of life anywhere in space remains at zero.

1908. Barnum Brown found one of the first complete *Tyrannosaurus Rex* fossils this week in Montana. He wrote, "The skull alone is worth a summer's field work for it is perfect." The second *T. Rex* specimen was located in 1966, nearly 60 years later. Another *Tyrannosaurus* fossil from South Dakota sold for $8.4 million at a 1997 auction.

About a dozen specimens now are known, all from the western states and Canada. These fossil remains reveal a warmer, tropical world in the past. Dinosaurs actually were created on the fifth and sixth days of creation, when sea and land animals first appeared.

T. Rex *skull*

August 9

This time of year the earth passes through a cloud of debris in its annual orbit around the sun. As the pebble-size particles fall through the upper atmosphere they burn up and make a temporary streak of light across the night sky. These "shooting stars" comprise the Perseids meteor shower, and can be seen for several nights. The space fragments are fragments from a comet called Swift-Tuttle. Space debris reminds us that comets, and solar system objects in general, do not last forever.

August 10

1846. The Smithsonian Institution was founded today by the official signature of James K. Polk, 11th president of the United States. British scientist James Smithson financed the initial project although he never came to America. The museum's purpose is to be for the "increase and diffusion of knowledge among men." The Smithsonian houses a wonderful display of creation examples from around the world, along with man's inventions. The frequent evolutionary explanations in the exhibits cannot obscure the real message of creative design.

August 11

1877. This evening Asaph Hall was exploring Mars with the U.S. Naval Observatory telescopes. He succeeded in finding a small moon circling the planet, later named Deimos. A week later Hall found a second Martian moon, named Phobos. He honored his wife for the discovery: "The chance of find-

Mars

Diemos

ing a satellite appeared to be very slight, so that I might have abandoned the search had it not been for the encouragement of my wife."

Phobos

Over 60 planetary moons are now known throughout the solar system. However, our own moon is unique in its provision of evening light, tides, and eclipses. Astronomers have been unable to successfully explain the origin of any planetary moons.

1799. An important archaeology discovery occurred sometime this month. French troops were stationed in Egypt during one of Napoleon's military invasions. He brought with him scholars

AUGUST
12

whose purpose was to survey the ancient monuments of Egypt. While repairing a fort near the town of Rosetta, soldiers found an engraved stone in the ruins of an old wall. The black basalt tablet, dating to 200 B.C., was about 4 feet by 5 feet in size and carried many lines of text in three writing systems: hieroglyphics, demotic script (a cursive form of hieroglyphics), and Greek. Until this time no one was able to read Egyptian hieroglyphics. The Rosetta Stone allowed translation of the hieroglyphics which are found all over Egypt. Hieroglyphics form the earliest known written language, about 5,000 years old. Multiple languages originated at the Tower of Babel dispersion as described in Genesis 11, perhaps including early forms of writing.

AUGUST 13

On Venus, our nearest neighboring planet, today is the last day of the year. Venus completes a trip around the sun in 225 earth days. Venus is earth's twin in size but is completely opposite in many other ways. Its surface temperature, due to a runaway greenhouse effect, is a constant 880°F (472°C). Venus clouds consist of carbon dioxide and sulfuric acid. The surface air pressure is a crushing 90 times greater than that of earth. One reason for the creation of our neighboring planets is surely to teach us that there is no other place like home.

1820. The first permanent eye hospital opened today in New York City. It began as a small clinic with just two surgeons. The human eye clearly shows creative design. The delicate eyeball is recessed in its socket for protection from

AUGUST 14

injury. Involuntary blinking keeps the outer cornea moist and clean, somewhat similar to an automobile's windshield washer and wipers. Dual eyes allow us to see depth in three dimensions. Our eyes also are found to heal very quickly from injury or corrective surgery. Eye banks are now a part of many modern hospitals worldwide. The demand for donated eyes remains far greater than the available supply. Truly, the human body is priceless in value, including our eyesight.

AUGUST 15

1914. The Panama Canal was formally opened to ship traffic today. This 51-mile (82 km) channel provides direct passage between the Caribbean Sea and the Pacific Ocean. The engineering feat took ten years to complete, cost $400 million, and employed 43,400 construction workers. The total material excavated was 200 million cubic yards. In contrast, the Creator quickly removed ten trillion cubic yards of soil and rock in making the Grand Canyon during the Genesis flood era. This Arizona canyon is equal to 50,000 Panama Canals!

AUGUST 16

1771. In earlier times it was thought that plants were nourished exclusively by the soil. Joseph Priestley began experiments this week which showed that plants also "breathe," taking in carbon dioxide from the air. Priestley put a sprig of mint into a closed container in which a wax candle had used up the oxygen and had burned out. Ten days later, another candle easily burned in the same enclosed air. The mint had clearly converted carbon dioxide to oxygen. This is an opposite process from air-breathing creatures like ourselves who take in oxygen and exhale carbon dioxide. Priestley thus showed that vegetation constantly replenishes the atmosphere. Further studies have shown that over half of the earth's oxygen is generated by plants within the oceans.

AUGUST 17

1896. Gold was discovered today in Canada's Yukon Territory. Soon more than 30,000 miners poured into the Klondike region seeking their fortune. Fewer than 1 in 100 ever found gold.

Job 28 describes the strenuous efforts of men to find wealth inside the earth. They tunnel into the darkness of the earth and seek treasure there. Job further explains that true wealth and wisdom come from knowing the Creator who made the earth including all of its gold (see January 24).

AUGUST 18

1868. During a solar eclipse today a new element was discovered on the sun. Joseph Lockyer noticed a yellow line in the solar spectrum that could not be identified. The spectrum of light reveals several properties of the light source, including its chemical makeup. Lockyer named the element "helium" after the Greek name *helios* for the sun.

Twenty-eight years passed before helium was also found as a rare element in the earth's own atmosphere. Helium is now known to be the second most abundant element in the sun and other stars, after hydrogen (see October 27).

Solar eclipse

1874. John Tyndall (1820–1893) was a leading scientist in England and also president of the scientific British Association. Today he gave a famous speech in which he attacked Christianity:

We claim, and we shall wrest from theology the entire domain of cosmological theory.

What is the result 125 years later? Creation still remains a refreshing alternative to the ever-changing origin theories of natural science. And the goal of replacing the creation story with naturalistic ideas has failed completely. Scientist John Tyndall should not be confused with William Tyndale who translated Scripture into English during the reformation period.

1897. British researcher Ronald Ross made a major medical breakthrough today. After 15 years of study he finally proved that mosquitoes transmit malaria to humans. Since that time the control of mosquitoes has greatly diminished human suffering from disease. Ross was a physician and also a Christian poet. One of his poems describes the discovery:

AUGUST 20

> This day relenting God
> Hath placed within my hand
> A wondrous thing; and God be praised.

Research continues on a possible vaccine that might someday eliminate malaria altogether.

AUGUST 21

1875. A great cloud of locusts passed over the state of Nebraska this week. Called Rocky Mountain locusts, the swarm was the greatest concentration of insects ever recorded in modern history. These insects covered an area the size of Colorado and Oregon combined. There were at least 12.5 trillion locusts, weighing a total of

27.5 million tons. This insect pest disappeared completely by 1902 and has not been seen since. The 1875 event is similar to the locust plagues recorded in the Old Testament. A sudden population explosion of insects may occur when ecological systems become unbalanced in either competition or food supply. In contrast, the plague of locusts which long ago occurred in Egypt was a supernatural event (Exod. 10:14). This Old Testament locust invasion was even more severe than the 1875 event in the United States.

1982. President Ronald Reagan today made a statement that created major ripples in the media. He remarked that he "had a great many questions" about evolution, which was "only a theory [and] not believed in the scientific community to be as infallible as it was once believed . . . discoveries down through the years have pointed out great flaws in it." There was much popular support for Reagan's wise words. However, anyone who voices such sentiments in public is in peril. The president was quickly labeled an anti-evolution fundamentalist by the press.

1984. A discovery was made today in Kenya by Richard Leakey. The skeleton of a young boy 9 to 11 years old was found and dated at 1.6 million years old. This *Turkana Boy* was about five feet tall, with very human proportions. He was classified as *Homo erectus*, an extinct ancestor of modern man. There is still no evolutionary agreement on whether Homo erectus was our direct ancestor or a separate branch of life. In the creation view the Turkana Boy is not distinguished from a modern person. His lifetime was sometime during recent biblical history. Animals and mankind have always been in distinct categories since their creation.

A.D. 79. A volcanic eruption today completely destroyed the Roman cities of Pompeii and Herculaneum in Italy. Ash from Mount Vesuvius quickly buried both cities and killed 20,000 citizens. The region was largely forgotten for a thousand years, then excavated in 1748. Modern archaeology is said to begin with this initial Italian research. Pliny the Younger recorded a vivid account of the actual explosion:

> [It was] as if the lamp had been put out in a closed room. . . . You could hear the shrieks of women, the wailing of infants, and the shouting of men. . . . [Some] prayed for death in their terror of dying. Many besought the aid of the gods, but still more imagined there were no gods left, and that the universe was plunged into eternal darkness.

One can imagine the terror of the final biblical judgment upon the lost, when the Creator cleanses his entire earth with fire as described in 2 Peter 3:10–12.

1989. The *Voyager II* space probe finally reached the vicinity of planet Neptune today after traveling outward from the earth for 12 years, a distance of 2.8 billion miles. The probe transmit-

Neptune

ted back to earth the first detailed pictures of faraway Neptune. This planet is a light blue color with white wispy clouds. As with the other large outer planets, there is no solid crust, but instead Neptune is a gaseous sphere. No other planet yet discovered has the needed conditions for life as providentially provided on the earth.

AUGUST 26

1883. One of the greatest explosions in earth history occurred today. Krakatoa, an island volcano near Java in Indonesia, violently erupted. The explosive sounds were heard even in Australia, 3,000 miles (5000 km) away. Volcanic dust circled the globe for two years before settling, and cooled the entire earth by several degrees. In Java, 200 towns were destroyed and about 40,000 people were drowned by resulting tidal waves, or tsunamis. A little more than a century later, the nearby islands are once again covered with lush tropical vegetation. The earth has been created with strong and rapid recovery capabilities.

AUGUST 27

1859. Oil gushed out of the first commercial well today near Titusville, Pennsylvania, drilled by Edwin Drake. Twenty barrels were produced per day, thus beginning a great oil boom in the eastern states. Along with natural gas and coal, oil is a fossil fuel which results largely from buried plant material. Much of this vegetation probably grew in preflood times and was buried in the great flood catastrophe. The fossil fuels are thus a useful inheritance from the preflood world.

1932. The first *antimatter* was made this month using a particle accelerator in California. The short-lived trail of a high speed *positron* was identified. A positron is exactly like an electron but with a positive charge instead of negative. When an electron and positron collide, they annihilate each other and produce an x-ray. There is thus an elegant symmetry to the created particles of the universe. One version of the big bang theory requires equal amounts of atoms and anti-atoms to exist in the universe. However, antimatter appears to be quite rare in space, in conflict with this particular natural origin theory.

1831. Today Michael Faraday experimented with wires and batteries. His journal describes an electric circuit which caused changes in the current of a separate nearby circuit. In this way Faraday had discovered the principle of the electric transformer. Millions of these devices today make electrical transmission possible around the world. Natural electrical currents are widespread in the creation. They generate the earth's magnetism and also cause the aurora, or northern lights. Tiny internal electrical currents also regulate the functions within our bodies (see April 8).

1979. Space cameras today recorded a comet colliding with the sun. The ball of frozen gases disappeared almost instantly and produced the energy of one million hydrogen bombs in the process. Comets are temporary members of the solar system. All of them eventually melt,  collide with other space objects, or sometimes escape the sun's grasp altogether. The continued existence of many comets is an indication of a recently created solar system.

 1735. During church services today, lightning struck the meeting house in New London, Connecticut. Several people were injured and one parishioner was killed by the explosive energy. The Reverend Adams later published a related sermon with the title, "God Sometimes Answers His People by Terrible Things in Righteousness," taken from Psalm 65:5. During this colonial era God's power and glory were greatly respected. Adams told his congregation:

> We should stand in awe of Him when He thus loudly utters His voice. For there was need of something very awakening to rouse us out of that deep security, into which many of us were fallen.

1914. This date marks the death of the last known passenger pigeon. Her name was Martha and she had lived in the Cincinnati Zoo for 25 years. When pioneers crossed North America

a century earlier, the passenger pigeon was the most abundant bird. Flocks numbering a billion birds or more were not unusual. However, their number rapidly dwindled due to disease, loss of food supply, and widespread hunting. The rapid demise of the passenger pigeon follows a common pattern in nature. The fossil record shows that over 90 percent of the original created plants and animals have been lost over time. The living world today is greatly impoverished, a result of the curse upon nature and also historical changes in habitat. This loss of plants and animals is in direct conflict with the assumed evolutionary development of increasing varieties of life forms over time.

SEPTEMBER 2

1752. Great Britain and the American colonies declared that September 14 would directly follow today, erasing September 3–13 completely from the 1752 calendar. The correction was needed to bring the calendar back into alignment with the seasons. Pope Gregory had established the revised calendar in 1582 but many countries were slow to adopt the change (see October 13). Japan finally dropped the extra days in 1873, and Russia did the same in 1918. Many people didn't understand this calendar correction and believed that the days somehow had been subtracted unfairly from their lives. The calendar adjustment shows how complex and important timekeeping is to mankind.

SEPTEMBER 3

1821. A strong hurricane moved through the New England states today. These storms occur rather frequently, but this time meteorologist William

Redfield noticed something different. From the pattern of fallen trees he concluded that the winds had a spiral motion. Redfield had discovered that storm winds whirl counterclockwise when north of the equator. In general, low pressure air masses rotate in this direction while high pressure cells rotate clockwise. These wind directions are exactly opposite in the Southern Hemisphere. The pattern is due to the earth's spinning motion, and these circulating air masses largely control the entire world's weather. A similar swirling effect is also observed in the atmospheres on other planets.

SEPTEMBER 4

1954. Weightlifter Peter Cortese set a new record today. During competition at York, Pennsylvania, he achieved a one-arm dead-lift of 370 pounds, over triple his body weight. In the dead-lift event, the weight is lifted to the level of the hips and then lowered again by controlled effort to the floor. Under such a load the body's bones are actually compressed by a measurable amount. The abilities of the created human body are amazing, with bone and muscle strength exceeding that of steel.

SEPTEMBER 5

1906. Scientist Ludwig Boltzmann (1844–1906) took his own life today. He was a pioneer in the study of gases and thermodynamics. In particular, Boltzmann described the second law of thermodynamics, by which all things deteriorate and become less ordered over time. Non-acceptance of his science ideas eventually led to Boltzmann's depression and suicide. Strangely, his death was the ultimate expression of the second law itself. Boltzmann's will requested that a mathematical formula representing the second law be placed on his tombstone. This unusual epitaph remains today in his homeland of Austria.

SEPTEMBER 6

1779. The name *oxygen* was first proposed by French chemist Antoine Lavoisier (1743–1794) this week. His studies had showed that this gas sustained life and was also responsible for combustion. Lavoisier is sometimes called the founder of modern chemistry for his many discoveries. Some scientists have proposed that oxygen developed gradually in the earth's atmosphere over a long time span. However, historical data clearly points to the permanent presence of oxygen on the earth. Oxygen is 21 percent abundant in our atmosphere and has been present since the beginning in order to sustain the life created here.

This French engraving shows Lavoisier combining hydrogen and oxygen with an electric spark to produce water.

1936. Boulder Dam, also called Hoover Dam, began producing electricity today. This impressive curved wall of concrete is 1,244 feet across and 660 feet thick at its base. It blocks the Colorado River, forming Lake Mead with 800 miles of shoreline. The dam generates hydroelectric power, prevents flooding, and provides a permanent water supply to the region. The colossal size of this project shows the mighty efforts needed to control a single river. Meanwhile, every day, the created hydrologic cycle operates across the entire earth.

SEPTEMBER 7

SEPTEMBER 8

1900. A surprise hurricane slammed into Galveston, Texas, today. This time period was before the era of weather satellites, when such storms often struck without warning. As a result, more than 6,000 people perished as flood waters swept over the coastal Texas city. Aircraft and satellites today provide us with a helpful understanding and prediction of violent weather.

1977. The first TRS-80 computer was sold today. This was one of the earliest personal computers to find a large market. Affectionately known as a "Trash-80," its memory was small and it had no color or complex word processing capabilities. Computers today have millions of times greater memory capacity, and ten years from now our current computers will similarly be outdated. Meanwhile, *all* computers fall far short of our created minds.

SEPTEMBER 9

1910. Today a great forest fire roared across Idaho. The flames destroyed 3 million acres of timber, equal to a square area of forest 118 miles on each side. Over the centuries these great fires have repeated themselves, some caused by people and others by lightning. Each time the earth quickly has shown its created resiliency in its ability to recover from the damage. Although dangerous to living creatures in its path, fire is sometimes necessary to renew a forest.

The Surveyor 5 *lands on the moon.*

1967. The unmanned U.S. *Surveyor 5* space probe landed on the moon's surface today. It performed the first analysis of lunar soil. The moon soil contains silicate sand grains, similar to the earth, but no biological activity whatsoever. There is also no lunar atmosphere or liquid water. In contrast to the living earth, the moon is completely lifeless.

1758. Tonight French astronomer Charles Messier began to compose a list of unusual objects in the evening sky. He started with the Crab Nebula, a vast cloud of gas resulting from a star which exploded nine centuries ago. The Crab Nebula is now known as object number one in the Messier list, which eventually totaled 107 objects. Messier was a comet hunter and his list was compiled to avoid confusion with non-cometary objects. Today, Messier's list of galaxies, nebulae, and star clusters is of great interest to astronomers. This list shows the incredible variety of objects easily visible in the night sky.

1814. Francis Scott Key was aboard a ship tonight in Baltimore Harbor, watching the British attack on Fort McHenry. The next morning he saw the American flag still waving over the damaged fort. Francis then penned the words to the *Star-Spangled Banner*. The second verse is less familiar than the first. It honors the Creator of the world who has mightily blessed our land:

> Then conquer we must, when our cause it is just;
> And this be our motto: "In God is our trust!"

This song was declared to be the U.S. national anthem during the depression years of the 1930s.

SEPTEMBER 14

1963. Today the first surviving quintuplets were born in the United States. Mary Fischer of Aberdeen, South Dakota, gave birth to four girls and a boy. Many parents rightfully describe a single birth as a miracle. Quintuplets must then be a five-fold miracle! Multiple births have become more frequent in recent years with the use of fertility drugs and modern medical care.

SEPTEMBER 15

1620. This week 102 Pilgrims sailed from Plymouth, England, to the New World aboard the *Mayflower*. Separating from the Church of England, they sought freedom to worship their Creator as Puritans. Thirteen weeks later they landed at Plymouth Rock in present-day Massachusetts. Great sacrifice was made for religious freedom. Half the colony died during the first harsh winter. The *Mayflower Compact*, America's first written constitution, begins, "Having undertaken for the Glory of God, and Advancement of the Christian Faith . . . to plant the first colony in the northern parts of Virginia. . . ."

SEPTEMBER 16

1782. The Great Seal of the U.S. was displayed for the first time today, having been approved by Congress some months earlier. On the front is an American bald eagle bearing a ribbon with the phrase *E pluribus unum*, meaning one out of many. The reverse side shows an unfinished pyramid with the "eye of Providence" above it. This eye is said to represent the Creator's care and protection of the nation. The Latin words beneath the pyramid say, "He (God) has favored our undertakings." The Great Seal can be found on the reverse side of the one dollar bill.

SEPTEMBER 17

1940. Sometime this week, serious study began on early art work discovered in the French caves of Lascaux. Days earlier some boys found the cave entrance in brush while chasing their dog. The cave walls display some of the oldest paintings known. They picture bison, horses, ibexes, reindeer, and even a unicorn figure. Thousands of footprints are also preserved on the cave floor. The assumed occupation date of around 12,000 B.C. is suspect, but the artifacts surely date to early Old Testament times. The pictures show the abilities of early artists. The unknown individuals were not primitive savages, as our predecessors are often pictured. When the painter Pablo Picasso saw Lascaux he exclaimed, "We have invented nothing!"

SEPTEMBER 18

1965. Today the largest known living bird was measured and then released by the crew of an Antarctic research ship. This particular *wandering albatross* had a wingspan of 12 feet. The largest-ever flying creature in earth history was probably the pterosaur. This flying reptile had a wingspan greater than 40 feet and weighed over 250 pounds. The world has had many large and magnificent creatures, both in the past and present. Psalm 104, sometimes called the ecologist's psalm, describes life on earth:

> How many are your works, O LORD! In wisdom you made them all; the earth is full of your creatures (Ps. 104:24).

1991. Today a German couple was hiking in the Alps on the border of Austria and Italy. In a ravine they came upon a frightening sight, the frozen body of a man. Subsequent study showed the "Iceman" to be about 5,000 years old. Nevertheless, he was a well-equipped hunter and not at all primitive. He wore a cap of brown bear fur. Also found at the site were a bow with 14 arrows, flint knife, copper axe, birch bark container for carrying charcoal embers, rope, and a pouch of medical herbs. The clothing remnants showed precise seams; his body tattoos included two crosses. In the creation view, this hunter probably dates to the early centuries following the Tower of Babel dispersion (Gen. 11).

1954. The first computer program was run today using the Fortran programming language. Previously, all programming was done numerically. Fortran was the first higher level, English-oriented approach to writing computer programs. It was followed by hundreds of other computer languages including Cobol, Visual Basic, and C. There was one other time in history when languages rapidly multiplied, in that case by divine command at the Tower of Babel (Gen. 11).

1782. The first English language Bible in America was printed today by Robert Aitken of Philadelphia. The venture was authorized by the U.S. Congress. The preface reads, "The Holy Bible, containing the Old and New Testaments newly translated out of the original tongues; and with the former translations diligently compared and revised." America has always been blessed with free access to God's word. Genesis 1:1 is by far the most-read sentence in all of history.

SEPTEMBER
21

SEPTEMBER
22

1792. An experiment in timekeeping began today. France instituted the new French Republican Calendar. There were to be 12 months of 30 days each, and also the week was to be 10 days long. This change was intended to replace the traditional week with its biblical association. The French New Year began on this particular date in September. However, total confusion resulted with schedules, resulting in a return to the 7-day week just 14 years later! There appears to be something very basic about the normal seven-day week, first given to mankind at creation (Exod. 20:11).

• • • •

Around this date the sun crosses the earth's equator and moves into the Southern Hemisphere. This is called the first day of fall in the north and also the autumn equinox, a time of equal daylight and darkness for everyone on earth. Earth's seasons result from the 23.5° tilt of the earth's axis. Genesis 8:22 promises continued seasons:

> As long as the earth endures, seedtime and harvest, cold and heat, summer and winter, day and night will never cease.

1846. This evening the eighth planet, Neptune, was discovered by German astronomer Johann Galle. Neptune's existence and position had been predicted earlier by careful analysis of its outward gravity pull on the planet Uranus. This success shows the exact predictability of the created laws of motion. We commonly call them Kepler's or Newton's laws, but in reality they are the Creator's laws.

SEPTEMBER 23

SEPTEMBER 24

1960. This is an important date for the discovery of asteroids, when more than one hundred new objects were located in a single night. Most of these large space rocks orbit the sun in a belt between Mars and Jupiter. Many of the asteroids are miles in size, and contain various metallic elements. These objects would be very valuable if somehow they could be brought back to earth. There are many such treasures in space.

1513. Today Spanish explorer Vasco Nunez de Balboa crossed the Isthmus of Panama to reach the Pacific Ocean. He thus claimed discovery of the world's largest ocean, twice the size of the Atlantic. The usually calm Pacific Ocean occupies about one-third of the earth's surface, more than the whole land surface of the globe.

• • • •

1922. This month a large fossilized egg was found in Mongolia's Gobi Desert by photographer J.B. Shackleford. Instead of a bird egg, it was that of a dinosaur. Over the years this desert area has produced a large number of dinosaur and fossil eggs. Dinosaur eggs and accompanying nests show that dinosaurs had a complex family structure. They displayed parental care just as modern animals do.

1871. An important U.S. patent was filed today. Its informal description: "Mix limestone and clay, add water and throw in a few rocks, and you've got concrete. Skip the rocks and you've got hydraulic cement." This is the formula for cement production, and it also describes the origin of much of the earth's sedimentary rock. Examples include limestone, sandstone, and shale. The Genesis flood provided a watery environment for the formation of much of the sedimentary rock which today covers the land surfaces of the earth.

1905. Today Albert Einstein submitted a famous paper about relativity theory to the German journal *Annalen der Physik*. The article presents the well-known relationship between energy (E), mass (m), and the speed of light (c):

$$E = mc^2$$

Einstein thus explained that all matter is equivalent to vast amounts of energy. Under certain circumstances this mass can be converted to energy in the form of light, heat, sound, and motion. Einstein presented two other significant papers this same year, concerning the photoelectric effect and the constancy of the speed of light.

1869. Today for the first time, electricity was generated from a waterfall. This early generator was built in the French Alps to operate factory machines. Hydroelectricity now supplies power to many communities around the world. The Creator provides this clean, renewable energy source by causing the evaporation of water and its transport to high elevations. As the water moves back downhill it can be harnessed to produce electrical energy. There are multiple benefits provided by the movement of water in nature.

1859. American pioneers reported a great auroral display this evening. The beautiful northern and southern lights danced across the sky throughout the

night. These auroral displays result from solar wind particles that are swept toward the earth's poles by its magnetic field. As the particles descend they collide with atmospheric atoms, causing them to glow. For unknown reasons the sun has an 11-year cycle of activity. During this time period the sun passes through a minimum and maximum of solar wind emission. Years of maximum activity, good opportunities for seeing the aurora, are around 2001, 2012, and 2023 (see December 8).

SEPTEMBER 30

1861. This year an unusual bird fossil was found 20 meters below the surface in a Bavarian limestone quarry. It later was named *archaeopteryx*, meaning "ancient wing." The fossil came to the attention of the science world on this particular date when a descriptive letter was published. Naturalist Richard Owen described this "early bird" in a talk before the British Royal Society. For many years *archaeopteryx* was considered to be strong evidence for evolution. It was called a direct link between lizards and birds. However, its modern feathers and bone structure show *archaeopteryx* to be fully a bird in every sense. The multiple links between animal and plant types are still missing.

OCTOBER 1

Following the great flood of Noah, mountaintops first became visible today according to Genesis 8:5 — on the first day of the tenth month. This was 74 days following the start of the flood. Before Noah and his family could safely leave the ark, 297 additional days passed. From this literal description in Scripture, the flood was surely global in extent. The flood teaches us that God is very patient with mankind. However, a time of correction will surely come, sooner or later. In Noah's day the earth was cleansed with water. The final judgment will be with fire, when the elements themselves will melt with fervent heat (2 Pet. 3:10–12).

OCTOBER 2

1706. A new commentary on the Bible first appeared today, written by Matthew Henry. It was 2,000 pages long with 3 million words, and this project was accomplished long before computers and word processing were available. Henry wanted his book "to make the reading of Scripture more easy, pleasant, and profitable." Three centuries later this commentary still sells about 25,000 copies each year. Matthew Henry's comments continue to encourage serious Bible study, from Genesis through Revelation.

OCTOBER 3

A.D. 1226. This early date marks the death of St. Francis of Assisi (1182–1226). The remarkable man wrote much about his love for the creation. One of his poems appearing in our hymnals is titled *All Creatures of Our God and King*. This hymn describes the wind, sun, and water which God has made:

> Thou flowing water, pure and clean,
> Make music for thy Lord to hear.

According to tradition, the poem was begun in early July

St. Francis of Assisi

1225, during a time of pain and loss for St. Francis. He had given all his possessions to the poor and ministered to people afflicted with leprosy. His entire life was an expression of joy in both God and His created world.

1957. This fall evening a new light could be seen moving slowly across the night sky. The Russian *Sputnik*, "little traveler," became the first artificial satellite to orbit the earth and begin the Space Age. *Sputnik* lasted just 3 months before plunging back to earth and burning up. Since then thousands of other satellites have been launched. Each space vehicle shows the dependability of the created laws which govern satellite motion. Man-made satellites are always temporary. They eventually wear out and fall back to earth. There is only one permanent, natural satellite. This is our created moon which faithfully circles the earth 12 to 13 times each year.

Sputnik

OCTOBER 5

1923. On this night astronomer Edwin Hubble was exploring the Andromeda Galaxy with the new 100-inch Mount Wilson telescope. Within Andromeda he noticed a particular type of star called a Cepheid variable. Such stars reveal their distance by the way their light output periodically changes. Hubble was thus able to determine the distance to Andromeda Galaxy for the first time. It was the greatest distance then known in space. Andromeda today is estimated to be 2.9 million light years away from the earth, yet this is actually a nearby galaxy.

OCTOBER 6

1995. Astronomers today reported the discovery of a planet orbiting another star, called 51 Pegasi, 40 light-years outward from the solar system. This new planet, if real, is far different from earth. Its surface temperature is more than 1000°C, and it must be gaseous like Jupiter. Many other possible planets have also been detected around other stars. However, it is doubtful that another earth-like planet will ever be found, and it is certain that no evolved life will be found on any planet, anywhere in space. The probability of the spontaneous origin of life remains at zero.

1959. For the first time today, the Russian spacecraft *Luna 3* sent back pictures of the far side of the moon. Because of the moon's equal rotation and revolution periods, the far side is never seen from the earth. For many years there was speculation as to hidden features

OCTOBER 7

and perhaps even lunar beings on the hidden side of the moon. However, the pictures from *Luna* showed a moon surface littered with craters similar to the visible near side. New lunar features were named the Gulf of Cosmonauts, the Sea of Moscow, and the Sea of Dreams. The entire moon has a raw, unfinished appearance in contrast to the beautiful earth.

OCTOBER 8

1945. American inventor Percy Spencer today patented the first microwave oven. Electron magnetron tubes which generated microwaves already were being used for radar defenses. Spencer noticed that the tubes also produced considerable heat in nearby water containers. As an early application, he made popcorn in a paper bag! Microwaves are part of the electromagnetic spectrum, first created when God said according to Genesis 1:3, "Let there be light."

1677. Dutch scientist Anton van Leeuwenhoek (1632–1723) had spent years designing and building microscopes. Today he sent an important letter to the Royal Society of London describing some of his findings: "In the year 1675 I discovered living creatures in rainwater, which had stood a few days in a new earthen pot." Scientist van Leeuwenhoek had observed the important microscopic units of life which surround us. His letter was titled "Observations . . . Concerning Little Animals." The microscope has shown us the beautiful, complex details of creation on the small scale.

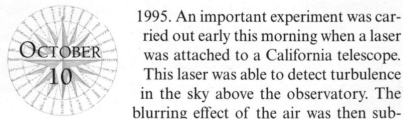

1995. An important experiment was carried out early this morning when a laser was attached to a California telescope. This laser was able to detect turbulence in the sky above the observatory. The blurring effect of the air was then subtracted from the telescope, a technique called adaptive optics. No longer did the earth's atmosphere distort the telescope image, a long-standing problem. This success means that many earth-based telescopes may eventually become equal to the Hubble Space telescope in observing power. Astronomy progress continues at a rapid pace as we learn more about deep space, where most of the creation is located.

1883. Railroad managers today adopted a plan to divide the United States and Canada into standard time zones. The local times kept by various cities had simply become too complicated for cross-country train schedules.  This new clock adjustment allowed noon to occur when the sun was highest in the sky, at all locations. Later these time zones were extended all around the world. There are now 24 such zones, each covering 15 degrees of longitude.

 1492. A lookout sailor for Christopher Columbus first sighted land at 2 a.m. this morning in the present-day Bahamas. The crew of 88 men had traveled through unknown seas for 42 days. Columbus was quick to give God the credit for his success in discovering the new world. He wrote, "God made me the messenger of the new heaven and the new earth. . . . He showed me where to find it" (see August 3).

1582. This day and nine other days were missing entirely from the calendar in 1582. Pope Gregory XIII had decreed that October 15 should directly follow October 4. The purpose was to realign the calendar with the seasons. A discrepancy had accumulated because of too-frequent insertion of extra leap year days in previous centuries. People protested this calendar adjustment, wrongly thinking that ten days had somehow been subtracted directly

from their lives! Periodic calendar corrections have been needed throughout history. The year 1582 had 345 days, and 45 B.C. had 80 extra days for a year total of 445 days. The latter was called "the year of confusion!" The Creator made us with both a curiosity and an ability to keep exact time.

OCTOBER 14

1947. Test pilot Chuck Yeager today became the first person to fly faster than the speed of sound in level flight. At an altitude of 42,000 feet this speed is about 670 miles per hour. Some skeptics had feared that achieving the speed of sound was impossible, or that it might prove fatal to the pilot. However, military planes now regularly fly more than 2,000 miles per hour, several times the speed of sound. Land vehicles have also exceeded the speed of sound. The engineering feats that God has granted to mankind to achieve high speed are truly a marvel.

OCTOBER 15

1838. Charles Darwin wrote this month that he had read for amusement an essay *On the Principle of Population* by Thomas Malthus. Malthus argued that human and animal populations always outgrow their food supply. This then leads inevitably to competition and eventual mass starvation. Malthus assumed that populations always grow geometrically (2, 4, 8, 16, 32, etc.) while food supplies, at best, grow arithmetically (2, 4, 6, 8, 10, etc.). This idea is falsified today by the dual trends of decreasing population growth and increasing food production. However, Darwin was strongly influenced by the pessimistic views of Malthus. Darwin used the faulty population ideas in his theory of natural selection, or competition for survival.

OCTOBER 16

1989. An important agreement was reached today by international traders. The Endangered Species Act banned the buying and selling of ivory. This hard, smooth protein material called dentin comes largely from the elephant's tusk. Dentin consists largely of calcium carbonate, $CaCO_3$. It has long been highly prized for carvings. In recent decades the demand for ivory has threatened the survival of African elephants. The law is an attempt to protect these and other ivory-bearing creatures. The creation viewpoint supports the protection of plants and animals that are endangered, at least within reasonable limits. God loves His creatures, according to Job 38–39, and so should we. God also has made us managers or caretakers of creation, including the animal world (Gen. 1:26).

OCTOBER 17

1929. The Russian government this month attempted to eliminate weekends! A new calendar was implemented with only five days each week, Monday through Friday. This calendar was an attempt to dissociate timekeeping from any religious bias, including the creation week. However, Soviet people enjoy weekends like everyone else, including a day of rest and worship for believers. This unpopular Soviet calendar was abandoned after only three years. The seven-day week, a direct reflection of the creation event, cannot be avoided (see September 22).

October 18

1967. Today the planet Venus was visited by two space probes within hours of each other. The Russian probe *Venera 4* never reached the Venus land surface. Instead, severe air pressure and a temperature near 900°F quickly destroyed the descending probe. Meanwhile, the U.S. probe *Mariner 5* detected an atmosphere of sulfuric acid and carbon dioxide. This probe survived the descent but lasted only hours on the surface of Venus. Venus is earth's twin in size and just 30 percent closer to the sun. However, its inhospitable conditions show how carefully prepared the earth is for life.

October 19

1807. Sir Humphrey Davy today announced his discovery of the element sodium. It was later given the symbol Na, from Latin. This is a soft, low-melting metal with nearly the same density as water. Known as the founder of chemistry, along with Robert Boyle, Davy made many discoveries with the help of assistant Michael Faraday. As with all elements, sodium is of great interest in medicine and technology. Sodium compounds are manufactured in millions of tons annually including common salt ($NaCl$), baking soda ($NaHCO_3$), and sodium hydroxide ($NaOH$). Every element in nature has specific properties and purposes.

October 20

1948. Swiss engineer Georges de Mestral doesn't remember the exact date this October when he walked his hunting dog in the woods. Arriving back home he noticed cockleburs in his socks and also in the dog's fur coat. These are round seed pods with a prickly surface which readily clings to fur or clothing. Closer inspection showed tiny hooks on the ends of the burrs which firmly attached to many surfaces. In this way their seeds are dispersed. From this finding de Mestral invented the Velcro fastener made of tiny nylon hooks and loops. Velcro is listed as one of the most useful inventions of the past century. The fastener is widely used in clothing, industry, and even medicine. Actually, the Velcro idea has been around as long as the created cockleburs. Bird feathers also show this same fastener design in their connecting side vanes.

1821. Michael Faraday published an important article today which described the first electric motor. With no formal schooling or mathematics knowledge, Faraday nevertheless became one of the great experimental scientists of all time. He built many electrical devices including magnetic coils, generators, and motors. Faraday was a conservative Christian who honored the Creator throughout his life (see April 8).

OCTOBER 21

OCTOBER 22

1844. According to religious leader William Miller (1782–1849) the world was supposed to end today. Many of his followers, called Millerites, disposed of their possessions and climbed to high places to await the Lord's return. Miller had based his prediction on a faulty view of biblical prophecy. For his disciples this became known as "the day of great disappointment." Throughout history there have been many attempts to guess the exact day of the Lord's return. The Creator may return to earth at any time, but date setting is warned against in Mark 13:32.

4004 B.C. John Lightfoot (1602–1675) suggested that Adam and Eve were created on this date. Lightfoot was an eminent Hebrew scholar and vice-chancellor at Cambridge University in England. His chronology was somewhat speculative although it reveals an earlier time when Bible study was a vital part of university scholarship. In recent years Lightfoot's creation date has been the object of much derision. However, he should be commended for holding to a supernatural creation, regardless of the suggested date. Lightfoot was certainly closer to the truth than the multi-billion year speculations for the natural origin of the universe.

OCTOBER 23

OCTOBER 24

1924. Today the U.S. Federal Bureau of Investigation officially began using fingerprints for identification. These prints are uniquely different for every person, including identical twins. If a fugitive attempts somehow to distort his fingerprint, new skin will eventually restore the original pattern. Fingerprints show that every person truly is a unique creation. Recent studies have shown that the pattern within a person's iris, the colored portion of the eye, can also be used for unique identification.

For many years this part of October has been designated as International Whale Watching Week. The idea began in Hawaii, since October is the prime season for whale watching in the Pacific Ocean. Whales are the largest creatures in the creation, weighing much

more than dinosaurs and elephants. Whales are also among the first creatures made according to Genesis 1:21:

> So God created the great creatures of the sea and every living and moving thing with which the water teems, according to their kinds, and every winged bird according to its kind.

There is a popular idea that life first began as a tiny protoplasm in the sea. Instead, however, the Creator began with the largest creature that has ever lived!

1785. An unusual gift arrived today at the port of Boston, having been shipped from Spain. The king of Spain sent George Washington two male donkeys. The purpose was to breed them with female horses (mares) to produce America's first native mules for farm work. Ever since, mules have carried burdens for farmers, travelers, and miners.

The mule itself cannot produce any further offspring. The biblical "kinds" described in Genesis 1 define the separate categories of creatures. The mule's sterility shows a built-in limit to genetic variation (see April 17).

1859. An important talk was presented today at the Berlin Academy by Gustav Kirchhoff. He announced that dark  lines had been discovered in the spectrum of sunlight. These dark lines resulted from light absorption by particular chemical elements in the solar atmosphere. Since each element has a distinct dark line "fingerprint," the composition of the sun and also faraway stars could now be determined. Thus were born the sciences of spectroscopy and astrophysics. Although we cannot travel to the remote stars, the Creator has given us methods by which we can study their properties. Star composition, motion, size, magnetism, and temperature can all be learned from light spectra (see August 18).

 1639. Harvard is the oldest university in the United States, founded today in Boston and named for clergyman John Harvard. The school began, like Yale and Princeton, to train pastors. First-year courses included logic, physics, Greek, Hebrew, rhetoric, botany, and theology. Here are some original entrance requirements for Harvard students (see May 9):

The student shall be able to decline perfectly the paradigms of nouns and verbs in the Greek tongue. Everyone shall so exercise himself in reading Scriptures twice a day that they shall be ready to give an account of their proficiency therein.

Students shall publicly repeat sermons in the Hall whenever they are called forth.

••••

1915. Sir Ernest Shackleton taught a valuable lesson today to his crewmembers. He and 29 men had just abandoned their ship *Endurance* after it was crushed in Antarctic ice. They had hoped to eventually cross Antarctica on foot, but suddenly their survival was at stake with the loss of their ship. Only barest essentials could be kept as the men began a 20-month odyssey of riding on drifting ice and hiking. By way of example, Shackleton on this day took the ship's Bible and tore out only one page for keeping, then laid the book on the ice. The verses he saved were from Job 38:29–30:

> Out of whose womb came the ice? and the hoary frost of heaven, who hath gendered it? The waters are hid as with a stone, and the face of the deep is frozen (KJV).

These words showed that God was with the men, even at the South Polar end of the earth. Every last man was eventually safely rescued by whaling ships. It was later learned that one of the explorers had secretly picked up the Bible and kept it for the entire time. It is now on display in London.

1929. Today marks Black Tuesday, when prices collapsed on the New York Stock Exchange amid panic selling. The fortunes of many investors were erased overnight. The 1930s became a decade of worldwide unemployment and economic depression. By 1932 one quarter of American workers were unemployed. World trade slumped by 57 percent during 1929–1936. Meanwhile, the Creator who seeks to care for us owns "the cattle on a

OCTOBER
29

thousand hills" (Ps. 50:10). We are only stewards of our possessions for a short time.

1938. Orson Wells played an ingenious trick on nationwide radio listeners tonight. The Sunday program began with simple dance music. Then suddenly a news reporter broke in, "Ladies and gentlemen, we must interrupt to bring you a special bulletin." He then described a fictional invasion taking place by Martians. Six million frightened people listened to the broadcast, and general panic resulted.

It was all a hoax, based on an 1895 British novel by Herbert G. Wells, *The War of the Worlds*. In the original novel, the Martians are eventually slain by bacteria, the "humblest things that God in his wisdom had put upon this earth."

Life in space is of great interest. Scientists continue to search for intelligent signals from space. Unfortunately, much of the motivation concerns evolution. Many are convinced that life evolved spontaneously on earth. And if so, it surely must have happened on other worlds as well. In spite of spending many millions of dollars, no such evidence has ever been found beyond the earth.

Halloween had its origin in the Druids of the British Isles thousands of years ago. Druids were a priestly cult with Celtic people as followers. On this day bonfires were lit to drive away the powers of darkness. Sacrifices were also offered to friendly gods. Many Celtic people

became Christians in more recent centuries. October 31 was first changed to a feast day, then became "All Saints Evening." Today's Halloween traditions seem to have returned to the early emphasis on the dark powers of darkness. Unfortunately, evil powers now are often welcomed instead of being driven away.

• • • •

1517. This date is sometimes called the "Fourth of July of Protestantism." It was today when Martin Luther (1483–1546) nailed his 95 theses to the door of the cathedral of Wittenberg, Germany. These writings condemned various unbiblical practices of the early Roman Catholic Church. Luther also wrote many hymns, including "A Mighty Fortress Is Our God." Based on Psalm 46, this well-known hymn boldly declares Christ as Creator with power over time itself:

> Dost ask who that may be?
> Christ Jesus, it is He —
> Lord Sabbath His name,
> From age to age the same —
> And He must win the battle.

NOVEMBER 1

1512. After five years of work, Michelangelo's paintings today were unveiled on the ceiling of the Sistine Chapel in the Vatican. These magnificent frescoes include scenes of the creation and also the fall of man. Michelangelo had earlier completed the marble sculpture *David* (1501). His painting *The Last Judgment* appeared in 1541. The Renaissance period demonstrated great familiarity and respect for biblical topics.

NOVEMBER 2

1875. Archaeologist George Smith today presented an important paper to the London Society of Biblical Archaeology. He had located ancient tablets which gave a Babylonian account of creation. This creation story is known today as the *Enuma elish*. The document describes an ancient battle between the gods. The goddess Ti'amat is slain and she then becomes the earth's land and sea. How much more genuine and clear is the Genesis creation account (see December 3).

NOVEMBER 3

1960. The Nobel Prize in chemistry was granted today to Willard Libby. He pioneered the carbon 14 method for determining the age of objects by their radioactivity. There are basic problems with radiometric dating, but carbon 14 has proven useful to archaeologists. For example, the Dead Sea Scrolls were dated by carbon 14 and found to be truly ancient and accurate. They are a testimony to the preservation of God's word through the centuries (see November 27).

NOVEMBER 4

1922. Today the entrance to King Tutankhamen's tomb was discovered in Egypt by archaeologist Howard Carter. King Tut reigned as a child in Egypt during 1361–52 B.C., dying at the early age of 18. Found at his burial site were a solid gold coffin, burial mask, and numerous treasures of furniture and jewelry. This discovery shows the advanced culture and artistry present during this

Old Testament era. Since the beginning of time, mankind has displayed artistic ability as part of God's image.

1879. A little-known but important scientist died today of cancer at age 48. James Clerk Maxwell (1831–1879) had spent his life studying diverse subjects such as gyroscopes, Saturn's rings, and gas laws. However, his greatest contribution involved electromagnetic waves, or light waves. Albert Einstein, born the same year Maxwell died, said that Maxwell's work was "the most fruitful that physics has experienced since the time of Newton." Maxwell displayed a strong Christian faith and could quote extensively from the Bible. By the age of eight he already had memorized Psalm 119. Maxwell was both a man of science and a man of God.

1572. A brilliant star explosion was recorded tonight by astronomer Johann Kepler (1571–1630). Called a supernova, the dying star was located in the northern constellation called Cassiopeia. Its brightness lasted an entire year before fading, a testimony to the aging and eventual decay of all stars. Supernovae are quite rare. There has not been a similar recorded nearby event within the Milky Way Galaxy since 1572.

1631. Astronomer Johann Kepler (1571–1630) successfully predicted an unusual event which occurred today. The planet Mercury was to pass directly across the face of the sun. Such a transit of Mercury had not been previously recorded or predicted. Unfortunately, Kepler died a year before this transit took place. However, it was witnessed by many other astronomers. Transits show the exactness of the laws by which the Creator governs the planets. Kepler ended his book *The Harmonies of the World* (1619) with a hymn of praise to the Creator:

> I give thanks to thee,
> O Lord Creator,
> Who has delighted me
> With thy makings and
> In the works of thy hands.

NOVEMBER 8

1895. X-rays today were discovered by Wilhelm K. Roentgen (1845–1923), which he produced using a crude vacuum tube. By experimentation Roentgen noticed that the invisible radiation could pass directly through the wall of his laboratory. Within days of his announcement, doctors began using x-rays to see inside the human body and repair injuries. Roentgen received the 1901 Nobel physics prize for this discovery.

NOVEMBER 9

1676. Astronomer Olaus Roemer (1644–1710) made an important prediction for today. A solar eclipse was to take place, but would occur ten minutes later than calculated from earlier eclipses. The time delay involved the speed of light, which Roemer earlier had measured based on the orbiting moons of Jupiter. His eclipse prediction proved accurate; Roemer had succeeded in establishing the exact speed of light for the first time. Light travels at about 186,000 miles per second, or 300,000 kilometers/second. This is nearly a million times faster than sound travels.

••••

1853. Today began a study of sunspots by Richard Carrington (1826–1875). From a private observatory he carefully counted sunspots, or solar blemishes, over the following eight years. The results showed that the sun slowly turns or rotates. One rotation takes about 35 days at the sun's equator, and 25 days at the poles. Carrington thus showed that our sun must be gaseous rather than a solid sphere, to rotate unequally in this way. Rotation is a universal nature of stars just as it is for all the planets and their moons. The Creator has set all space objects into motion to provide stability for the universe. Without these motions, gradual large-scale gravity collapse and chaos would occur everywhere in the universe.

NOVEMBER
10

1871. Dr. David Livingstone (1813–1873) had been sent to Africa by the London Missionary Society. For 32 years this Scottish medical missionary brought the gospel to Africa's unknown interior and also worked to abolish slavery. In his travels Livingstone discovered Victoria Falls and Lake Nyasa. On this date, ill with malaria, Livingstone finally was located in Tanzania by journalist-explorer Henry Stanley. Livingstone had not been heard from for three years. Stanley delivered his famous greeting: "Dr. Livingstone, I presume?" Livingstone replied, "Yes, and I feel thankful that I am here to welcome you."

Livingstone died two years later among his African friends. His life demonstrates the resolve of pioneer missionaries to share the story of creation and the gospel with others in faraway places.

1957. A laboratory notebook for this date shows the initial idea of laser light. Patent credit was finally given in 1986 to a Columbia University graduate student, Gordon Gould, who had written the informal report. Lasers are now of immense value in many fields, including medicine and technology. This "harnessing of light" shows the designed usefulness of the details of nature.

NOVEMBER 11

NOVEMBER 12

1980. The U.S. *Voyager I* space probe reached Saturn today and transmitted to earth detailed pictures of this beautiful ringed planet. The spacecraft arrived at Saturn 3.5 years after its launch, continually traveling five times faster than a bullet.

Voyager showed that Saturn's rings are numbered in the hundreds. Some of the rings are intricately braided while others have small shepherd moons separating them. The complex system of rings shows the Creator's unending artistry.

• • • •

1981. The British journal *Nature* today reported an interesting quote from astronomer Fred Hoyle. He spoke at a conference in California and referred to evolution:

The rings of Saturn.

The chance that higher life forms arose by chance is comparable with the chance that a tornado sweeping through a junk-yard might assemble a Boeing 747 from the materials therein.

Hoyle went on to say he was at a loss to understand the widespread compulsion of biologists to ignore the impossibility of evolution. Hoyle refused to accept the supernatural creation alternative. Instead, his idea was that life somehow came to earth from outer space. Instead of solving the problem of the origin of life, Hoyle simply moved it outward from the earth.

1833. An unusual meteor shower occurred in the early hours this morning. Hour after hour the sky was filled with brilliant "shooting" or "falling" stars. The earth had passed through a vast cloud of rock fragments in space, some of which then burned up in our atmosphere due to frictional heating. Many people were terrified and a historian gave this description:

NOVEMBER 13

> The day of judgment was believed to be only waiting for sunrise. . . . Impromptu meetings for prayer were held in many places.

The earth's orbit passes through this particular cloud of debris every autumn, resulting in the "Leonid meteor shower." The particles originate from Comet Temple-Tuttle which passes through this region of space. The appearance of meteor showers is very unpredictable. Perhaps this year will provide us with an especially impressive display. It might give us a healthy dose of reality regarding the temporary heavens which will one day quickly pass away, according to 2 Peter 3:10–12 (see August 19).

NOVEMBER 14

Geologist Charles Lyell (1797–1875), whose birthday is today, popularized the phrase "the present is the key to the past" in his *Principles of Geology* (1830) Lyell proposed an ancient age for the earth. However, he struggled with the ideas of his friend Charles Darwin. He couldn't accept the evolution of man from animals because "it takes away much of the charm of my speculations on the past relating to such matters."

. . . .

1963. A new island appeared today off the coast of Iceland. In the morning a fisherman noticed dark smoke rising from the sea. By evening, volcanic debris had begun to form Island Surtsey, named for the mythological god of fire. Volcanism continued for the next 3.5 years to form the mile-size island. Soon the wind and waves carved out ancient-looking beaches of black sand. Birds then brought seeds and insects to the island. Grasses began growing within one month of the eruption. Vegetation and small animals also were rafted to Surtsey on mats of seaweed and quickly established themselves. Thus, the new island took on an appearance of mature age. Surtsey reminds us that the created earth is programmed to quickly heal its scars, and to provide a habitat for living creatures everywhere.

1719. Paper was a rare commodity in past centuries. On this date a French scientist, Rene-Antoine Reaumur, shared with the French Royal Academy his important observation from a walk in the woods:

NOVEMBER 15

> The American wasps form very fine paper. . . . They teach us that paper can be made from the fibers of plants without the use of rags and linens, and seem to invite us to try whether we cannot make fine and good paper from the use of certain woods.

Wasps build their paper nests by processing wood fibers in their stomachs. Today the similar chemical processing of fibers is the main source of our paper products. There is obviously much to learn from studying the details of creation.

••••

1946. Cloud seeding began today, from a chance discovery. Scientist V. Schaefer had found that dry ice particles, or frozen carbon dioxide, caused super-cooled water vapor to form snowflakes. He then dropped dry ice into a cloud from an airplane which triggered a small snowstorm. This process duplicates the formation of rain and snow from natural condensation nuclei in the atmosphere.

NOVEMBER 16

1974. A major attempt to contact life in space began today. Radio signals were broadcast outward from the Arecibo Radio Telescope. This radio telescope, the largest in the world, is located in Puerto Rico. The $60 million project was called the Search for Extraterrestrial Intelligence (SETI).

The first message of greetings from earth was beamed toward a globular star cluster in the Hercules constellation, 25,000 light years away. No reply is expected soon!

1959. The De Beers company of Johannesburg, South Africa, today manufactured the first synthetic diamond. Such artificial diamonds are very small and not of gem quality. The several million carats now produced each year are used mainly as industrial diamonds for cutting and grinding (a carat equals 200 milligrams). The larger, beautiful diamonds are made only by the Creator deep within the earth.

NOVEMBER 17

1820. The frozen continent of Antarctica was discovered today by U.S. Navy Captain Nathaniel Palmer. He and a crew had sailed southward months earlier from Connecticut. The vast frozen continent of Antarctica covers 5.4 million square miles, or 9.3 percent of the planet's surface. Most of the earth's freshwater exists as ice in Antarctica. Eventually its icebergs may be used to supply water to people worldwide. Engineers have considered ways to move mile-size icebergs across the ocean and then to melt them and transport their water to land. If such large-scale projects occur someday due to shortages of freshwater, the earth's climate itself might be altered.

• • • •

1929. Transatlantic communication was suddenly interrupted today. The problem began with an earthquake off the coast of Newfoundland. This quake caused a vast movement of sediment along the deep sea bottom. Moving at a speed of 50 miles per hour, this "turbidity current" snapped 12 thick metal cables lying on the sea ocean, one after the other, over a distance of 400 miles. Until this time, many geologists doubted the existence of such massive turbidity currents. After this event they realized the presence and incredible force of large-scale underwater movement of sediments. Such currents were probably present during the Genesis flood, completely reshaping the earth's surface.

• • • •

1989. The *Cosmic Background Explorer* (COBE) satellite was launched today. This instrument was later credited with measuring "space wrinkles," a slight variation in the temperature of space radiation. This temperature variation was further said to be responsible for the initial formation of matter in space. The discovery was credited as the "Holy Grail," or the final proof, of the big bang. The temperature of space actually has a variety of possible interpretations. A rapid, supernatural creation remains a valid alternative to the big bang.

1863. Abraham Lincoln delivered the Gettysburg Address today as he dedicated the national cemetery in Pennsylvania. It was some months after the great July 1–3 battle in which Union forces had won a major victory over the South. In the first sentence Lincoln stated that "All men are created equal." Abraham was a godly man, and the Creator sustained him through the dark days of the Civil War.

NOVEMBER 19

NOVEMBER 20

1911. The words of the song *America the Beautiful* were first published as a poem this week. Katherine Bates said she was inspired to write the words while viewing the countryside from the summit of Pike's Peak in Colorado. Her hymn is a testimony to the many glorious details in the creation, including these:

> spacious skies
> amber waves of grain
> purple mountain majesties
> shining seas

Each verse of *America the Beautiful* ends with a prayer that God will bless America and that freedom and godly living will endure.

1877. Thomas Edison today invented the phonograph which permanently stored sounds on a wax cylinder. Since then sound recording has advanced through vinyl records, magnetic tape, and digital recordings. Along with music and words, these devices bring many delightful, faraway sounds of creation to listeners, including ocean waves, tropical birds, and desert winds.

Thomas Edison's wax cylinder phonograph.

1990. One of the earth's largest optical telescopes was completed and received its "first light" this week. The Keck telescope is built on top of a dormant volcano called Mauna Kea in Hawaii. It has a 394-inch mirror made up of 36 segments precisely fitted together. The first image recorded was of a beautiful spiral galaxy called NGC 1232. Large instruments like the Keck telescope have greatly expanded our view of the creation in deep space.

1654. Blaise Pascal (1623–62) records this as the day of his conversion to Christianity. He wrote that he was influenced by the faithful testimony of his younger sister and also a particular sermon about self-inspection. Pascal became a young-earth creationist and

NOVEMBER 23

debated early scientists who assumed the earth was millions of years old. Pascal strongly believed that there is sufficient, convicting evidence in nature for those who seek belief in the Creator. This is in agreement with Romans 1:19–20, which states that God's creative work is clearly seen all around us.

NOVEMBER 24

1859. Charles Darwin's *On the Origin of Species* was first published today. Many of Darwin's ideas came during his Pacific travels aboard the H.M.S. *Beagle* during 1831–1836. Evolutionary theory today continues to be based largely on philosophy rather than fact.

One day before publishing his book, Darwin wrote to his brother Erasmus, "Concerning [the origin of] species, in fact the *a priori* reasoning is so entirely satisfactory to me that if the facts won't fit, why so much the worse for the facts, in my feeling." This implies that Darwin placed his personal belief in evolution above scientific data.

NOVEMBER 25

1864. Benjamin Disraeli (1804–1881) served for eight years as British prime minister. He is also considered the founder of England's modern Conservative Party. In a speech given today the statesman considered the nature of mankind:

> The question is this: Is man an ape or an angel? I, my lord, am on the side of the angels.

Disraeli realized that humans are an entirely separate creation from the animal world. Every biological observation and experiment reinforces this truth.

NOVEMBER 26

1863. A proclamation was issued this fall by President Abraham Lincoln. A national day of thanksgiving was to occur on the last Thursday of each November. The idea first began much earlier, in 1619, when settlers in Virginia set aside a day to give thanks for survival in their new homeland. Writer Sarah Hale influenced Lincoln to officially declare this special day in her letter which said:

> Let us be consecrated now to our Father in Heaven, for His bounteous blessing bestowed upon us, as a perpetual Day of Thanksgiving for the American people.

Lincoln's proclamation reads, in part:

> It has seemed to me fit and proper that God should be solemnly, reverently, and gratefully acknowledged, as with one heart and one voice, by the whole American people. I do therefore invite my fellow citizens in every part of the United States, and also those who are at sea and those who are sojourning in foreign lands, to set apart

and observe the last Thursday of November as a day of Thanksgiving and praise to our beneficent Father who dwelleth in the heavens.

Many other countries also honor the Creator with special days of thanksgiving; for example, Canada on October 12 and Columbia on June 5.

1947. This week archaeologists at Hebrew University negotiated the purchase of the Dead Sea Scrolls. Some time earlier, a Bedouin shepherd boy had tossed stones into a small cave near the northwest shore of the Dead Sea. Hearing pottery break, the boy explored the opening and found old leather rolls in clay jars. Searchers later recovered over 400 documents. The original owners had hidden them as the Roman army advanced against rebel Jews in A.D. 68. Much of the Old Testament is preserved on these

NOVEMBER 27

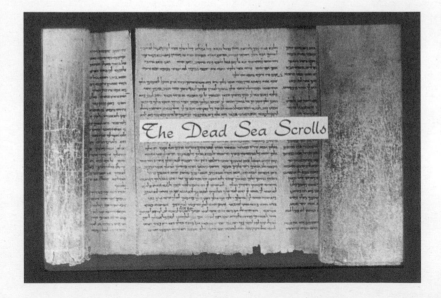

The Dead Sea Scrolls

important scrolls. Their close similarity to our present-day Bible shows how God has preserved the accuracy of His word over the millennia.

NOVEMBER 28

1967. Tonight British graduate student Jocelyn Bell detected an unusual radio signal from space. It varied or pulsed in intensity at a very regular rate of 1.3 seconds. Initially Jocelyn thought she had found signals from space beings. Her colleagues quickly named the object LGM, for "little green men"! Closer analysis revealed a new type of star, now called a pulsar. Hundreds of additional pulsars have been cataloged since 1967. These collapsed stars are rapidly spinning, some at hundreds of rotations per second. Their regular radio pulses are found to be the most accurate clocks known, even more precise than atomic clocks. Genesis 1:14 declares that the stars are useful for the keeping of days and years. Pulsars indeed appear to be the ultimate time standard.

1519. Explorer Ferdinand Magellan (1480–1521) today sailed into the quiet Pacific Ocean with five ships. He passed through the South American strait that now bears his name. This Strait of Magellan separates South America from other islands farther south in-

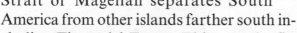

NOVEMBER 29

cluding Tierra del Fuego. This was the first expedition to sail completely around the world, giving positive proof that the world is round. The Pacific Ocean was found to be far larger than anyone had imagined, covering one-third of the earth's surface. Magellan sailed the Pacific for 98 days without seeing any land except two uninhabited islands.

1974. The nearly complete fossil skeleton of "Lucy" was found today by Donald Johanson in Ethiopia. The remains were named after the pop song "Lucy in the Sky with Diamonds" which was playing on a tape recorder at the researcher's campsite. The scientific name is *Australopithecus afarensis*. Johanson guessed that Lucy was a female and also that she walked upright. Thus, she became famous as a 3.2 million-year-old link from our evolutionary past. In truth, the date is controversial, and the jaws, teeth, and skull of Lucy are very ape-like. Lucy was probably a chimpanzee, and may have been either male or female.

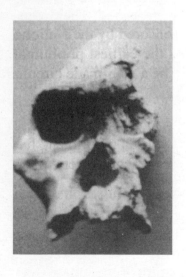

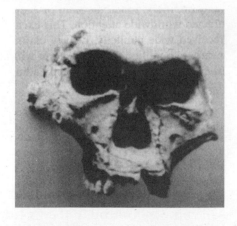

On the left is the skull of "Lucy." The skull on the right is "Skull 48," from Swartkrans in South Africa. For many years anthropologists claimed that the various forms of Australopithecines were transitional forms between apes and humans.

1958. The first color photo of the earth from the vantage point of space was recorded today by a rocket. The camera and data capsule actually were found two months later when they washed up on a Bahaman beach.

Since this time many thousands of spectacular space pictures have been taken of planet Earth. Each one shows how uniquely prepared the earth is for life, a blue-green oasis in the darkness of space.

1942. This day gave birth to the atomic age, with the controlled splitting of atoms. The first chain reaction of uranium occurred, supervised by physicist Enrico Fermi at the University of Chicago. This experiment brought the vast amount of energy within atoms under man's control. Sadly, nuclear accidents and weapons development have frustrated our efforts to enjoy this energy resource, a gift from the Creator.

• • • •

1982. Today the first artificial heart was implanted in volunteer patient Barney Clark by a team of doctors led by physician Dr. William De Vries. Clark lived for 112 days while the mechanical heart was kept operating with external power. Such pioneer experiments clearly show the created complexity of all parts of the human body, including the heart.

1872. An important report was given today to the London Society of Biblical Archaeology. Archaeologist George

Smith had located ancient stone tablets at Nineveh. The Babylonian story told on the tablets is known as the *Gilgamesh Epic*. Several additional copies of the story were later found in the ancient Near East. These flood traditions are not as reliable as the Genesis account. However they reveal a worldwide knowledge of the catastrophic event in the early centuries following the great flood (see November 2).

• • • •

1967. Today the first partially successful human heart transplant was performed by Surgeon Christiaan Barnard in Cape Town, South Africa. The patient, Louis Washkansky, lived with his new heart for 18 days. More than 2,000 such procedures now take place in the United States every year. For the cardiac patient in need, a healthy heart is more precious than all of earth's riches. Today almost 70 percent of heart transplant patients survive five years or more.

DECEMBER
4

1926. Albert Einstein wrote a letter today to his physicist friend Max Born, including a much-quoted statement. Einstein could not accept quantum theory, the idea that there is inherent uncertainty and chance in physical happenings. He wrote that "God does not play dice with the universe." Einstein may have had in mind Proverbs 16:33:

> The lot is cast into the lap, but its every decision is from the LORD.

When quantum theorist Niels Bohr later heard the quote, he remarked that Einstein should "stop telling God what to do." Quantum theory is an important topic in modern physics. However, happenings in nature which appear unpredictable to scientists remain completely known to the Creator. Uncertainty in science arises only from our limited understanding of reality.

1898. Sometime during early December of this year, Marie and Pierre Curie discovered the radioactive element radium. At this time the health dangers of radiation were not known. The Curie's recorded their work in notebooks which became contaminated, and are still radioactive a century later. In their honor the *curie* is now a measure of the radiation strength of one pure gram of radium. One curie amounts to 37 billion atomic disintegrations occurring each second. A single gram of pure radium can maintain this remarkable level of activity for centuries.

1884. During ceremonies today, an aluminum cap was set in place atop the Washington Monument. At this time pure aluminum metal was rare and was as valuable as gold. Aluminum actually is the most abundant metal in the earth's crust, but it does not occur naturally in its pure form. In 1886 an inexpensive method was found for separating aluminum from earth minerals using electricity. The Washington Monument is 555 feet tall with its once-rare cap in place. Engraved at the top, facing east, is the simple message in Latin, *Laus Deo*, "Praise God."

1981. During December 7–16, creation science was placed on trial in Little Rock, Arkansas. At issue was a new state law which required that balanced treatment be given in public school classrooms for creation and evolution views of origins. After much testimony on

both sides, Judge William Overton strongly ruled against creation teaching. His written document revealed a lack of understanding of the creation position.

• • • •

1995. After a six-year, 2.3 billion-mile odyssey the U.S. *Galileo* space probe finally reached Jupiter. Instruments on this date were parachuted deep into the planet's atmosphere. Some astronomers had hoped to find evidence for evolved life forms within the clouds of Jupiter. As usual, of course, they were greatly disappointed. Measurements revealed a lack of water, high temperatures, and poisonous gases. Winds blow at over 1,000 miles per hour. Jupiter is not a friendly place for life.

Jupiter

DECEMBER 8

1719. This week New England colonists observed an unusual display of lights in the night sky. The aurora borealis, or "northern lights," were recorded for the first time by settlers in North America. These beautiful lights result from solar wind particles (electrons, protons, and atom fragments) which become trapped in the earth's surrounding magnetic field. Magnetism is just one of several invisible shields which are designed to protect the earth from the hazards of space. Solar radiation is deflected magnetically to the far north or south where it then glows in the night sky (see September 29).

DECEMBER 9

1962. The Petrified Forest National Park of Arizona was established today, upgraded from a National Monument. This vast area contains 93 thousand acres of Indian ruins, petroglyphs, painted desert, and petrified trees. The original trees were buried underground where silica-containing water was present. The tree material was dissolved away and replaced by quartz, SiO_2. Beautiful minerals including jasper and agate result which perfectly outline the original tree rings. Much of the petrified wood found around the world may be a legacy of the Genesis flood upheaval.

DECEMBER 10

Each year. Nobel Prize presentation day occurs annually on this anniversary of the death of Alfred Nobel (1833–1896). The Swedish inventor earned a fortune through his discovery of dynamite. This chemical product changed the world by making possible massive building projects such as dams and tunnels. Dynamite also greatly raised the energy level of warfare. Nobel grieved over the loss of his younger brother who was killed during early experiments with explosives. Alfred Nobel's will established awards in peace, literature, and science "to those who, during the preceding year, shall have conferred the greatest benefit on mankind."

1900. During a lecture this week, physicist Max Planck introduced a new fundamental idea, known as the *quantum*. At a Berlin Physical Society meeting, he stated that energy does not occur in arbitrary amounts but instead always comes in discrete amounts or packets called *quanta*. Planck's presentation also described the wave-particle duality of light and quantum mechanics in general. This date sometimes is called the "birthday of quantum theory." A century later the quantum picture of nature continues to be studied and debated.

DECEMBER
11

DECEMBER
12

1901. Today is recognized as the birthday of the radio. The Italian engineer Guglielmo Marconi successfully broadcast radio waves across the Atlantic Ocean between England and Newfoundland. He used balloons to lift his antenna as high as possible. Radio waves travel at the speed of light. They are part of the useful and complex electromagnetic spectrum, which also includes visible light.

1920. This evening American astronomer Francis Pease measured the diameter of a nighttime star for the first time. He used an instrument called an interferometer to probe the star called Betelgeuse. This bright star in our December skies is found to be a giant, nearly a billion

miles in diameter, or about 1,000 times larger than the sun. The distance of Betelgeuse from earth is 520 light years, nearly three thousand trillion miles. The heavens are filled with stars and galaxies of all size. Genesis 1:16 gives the majestic understatement of God's creative power, "He also made the stars."

Betelgeuse is in the upper left shoulder of the constellation Orion (right).

DECEMBER
14

1911. Today the Norwegian explorer Roald Amundsen with four colleagues and dog teams reached the South Pole. December is the Antarctic summer season, but temperatures still plunge to -70°F. A year later Robert Scott also reached the South Pole, but none of his party survived the return. This hostile region of the earth illustrates the daily climate of frozen planets such as Mars and Pluto. Today there are permanent research centers in the Antarctic such as McMurdo Station, with hundreds of scientists doing climate research.

1791. The U.S. Bill of Rights became law today. This document consists of ten clarifying amendments to the Constitution. The first amendment concerns church and state: Congress shall make no law respecting an establishment of religion, or prohibiting the free exercise thereof; or abridging the freedom of speech, or of the press; or the right of the people peaceably to assemble, and to petition the government for a redress of grievances. This first amendment declares the freedom *of* religion, not a total separation of society *from* religion. Unfortunately this latter idea has become popular in our public schools and facilities, and society suffers as a result.

DECEMBER
15

DECEMBER
16

1811. The strongest earthquake in modern United States history occurred early this morning. It was centered at New Madrid, Missouri, near the Mississippi River. There were only scattered pioneers in the area at this time. Early diaries record the terror resulting from falling chimneys and groans from deep within the earth. Water, coal, and dinosaur bones were pushed upward out of the ground. Some areas of land in the Midwest sank downward, resulting in new lakes and swamps which still exist today.

There is a deep crack, or fault, in the earth's crust beneath Missouri, called the New Madrid fault. Many thousands of other such rock fractures occur all around the world. Tension gradually builds up on opposite sides of these fault lines. When slippage suddenly occurs, an earthquake results on the land surface above. It may be that many of these faults originated during the Genesis flood event. When the fountains or springs of the deep broke loose, subterranean water gushed upward. This was probably accompanied by earth-shattering volcanic activity. After the flood the ocean basins were supernaturally pushed downward and the continents upward according to Psalm 104:7–9, further fracturing the earth's bedrock. Many earthquakes occurring today may be distant aftershocks from the flood catastrophe.

1903. Today the Wright brothers flew their homemade airplane called *Flyer* for a distance of 120 feet at an altitude of 8-12 feet. At the time, only four American newspapers carried the story. Orville and Wilbur had long planned for this event near Kitty Hawk, North Carolina. By 1908, five years later, their flights were lasting an hour or longer. These early efforts were an attempt to duplicate the flying ability of birds. This natural display of bird flight first occurred on the fifth day of creation when birds were formed.

DECEMBER
17

The first flight to take off and land with its own power.

DECEMBER 18

1912. Today's newspapers carried an amazing headline: "Missing Link Found — Darwin's Theory Proved." The famous Piltdown Man fossil had been located in England. Over the next 40 years the pieces of skull and accompanying tools were studied, debated, and often used as evolution evidence. Four decades later however, in 1953, the artifacts were recognized as a complete fraud. Someone had placed together the skull of a human and the jawbone of an ape. They were artificially made to look old with acid and markings with a wire brush. The perpetrator has never been identified. Suspicions should have been raised immediately, for at least two reasons. First, Piltdown Man was found just 30 miles from Charles Darwin's residence. Second, one of the buried implements alongside the fossil strangely resembled a cricket bat used in modern British sports!

DECEMBER 19

1958. Today the first radio broadcast was transmitted from space. The U.S. satellite *Atlas* carried a recorded Christmas greeting from President Dwight Eisenhower. His 58-word message offered to the world "America's wish for peace on earth and goodwill toward men everywhere," a phrase taken from Luke 2:14.

DECEMBER 20

1969. This week the U.S. Air Force completed a thorough investigation of unidentified flying object (UFO) sightings. Called Project Blue Book, the study found that there was a lack of evidence for extraterrestrial spaceships. Many people have remained doubtful of the Air Force conclusion. There are indeed occasional unidentified objects in our skies. However, they are most likely man-made objects, weather phenomena, and in some cases, possibly tricks of Satan.

1872. Today the first oceanography ship set sail. The British *Challenger* began a two-year voyage to study the depths of the vast oceans. The trip was planned after a transatlantic cable was brought up from a one-mile depth in 1860 and found to be covered with unknown forms of plant and animal life. Suddenly the ocean depths became of great interest to biologists. During this first voyage, many metal nodules also were found resting on the ocean floor. The ocean depths remain a fascinating, secret part of creation.

DECEMBER 21

DECEMBER 22

This is the time of year for the winter solstice. Daylight now is shortest north of the equator and longest below, marking the official start of the northern winter, with summer beginning "down under." This seasonal change is due to the earth's tilt. Genesis 8:22 says there will be the faithful change of seasons, including seedtime and harvest, as long as the earth remains.

1975. The U.S. Congress declared today that the metric system was to become this country's basic system of measurement. Technical study of cre-

DECEMBER 23

ation details requires precise units of measurement, and laboratories around the world must agree on these units. The metric system includes meters, kilograms, and joules of energy. Meanwhile, the English system uses feet, pounds, and various energy units. Many people find it difficult to switch systems or to convert from one system to the other. Decades after the official change to metric units, they still are not popular in the United States.

DECEMBER 24

1938. This is a fish story. Today a most unusual creature was brought ashore in South Africa. The specimen had been caught in a net 240 feet deep, near the island of Madagascar off Africa's east coast. The deckhands described it as a "great sea lizard" because of its odd fins which looked somewhat similar to legs. Called a coelacanth, this fish was believed to have been extinct for 50 million years. Since 1938, many additional live specimens have been found. In 1997 they were also found swimming in Indonesian waters. Coelacanths average six feet long and weigh 150 pounds. They have been labeled "living fossils" because they continue to survive long after their supposed time period. In truth, the coelacanth is completely misunderstood by evolutionary science. It is a magnificent testimony to a recent creation, without extinction or any evolutionary change since the fifth day of creation.

• • • •

1968. Scripture was publicly read from space tonight. *Apollo 8* astronauts were circling the moon and sending back live television pictures to earth. Then there came a statement from Bill Anders, "For all the people of earth, the crew of *Apollo 8* has a message we would like to send you. In the

Apollo 8

beginning God created the heaven and the earth." Jim Lovell took up the reading, "And God called the light day, and the darkness He called night." Frank Borman completed the familiar verses, "And God called the dry land earth; and the gathering together of the waters called He seas: and God saw that it was good," taken from Genesis 1. There followed some protests over this Scripture reading, but many people were encouraged by the creation perspective of the early space program.

A.D. 440. This day was officially proclaimed as Christmas by the early church fathers. It was originally a Roman pagan holiday called Saturnalia, observed near the date of winter solstice. Actually, Christ probably was not born during the month of December. Shepherds do not ordinarily have their flocks in open fields

DECEMBER
25

after September, and it is doubtful that the Roman government would have required census travels during the winter season. Whether in spring or fall, the exact date of Christ's birth is not important. The Creator *did* come to bring us life, and that is what we celebrate at Christmas.

• • • •

1758. In Edmund Halley's day comets were mysterious visitors in the night sky. Many people thought that comets were supernatural omens of evil on the earth, but Halley thought otherwise. He realized that a 1682 comet was similar in appearance to historical records of former comets from the years 1531 and 1607. Noticing a period of about 76 years between these visits, he predicted a return of this same comet in 1758. At year's end on Christmas evening, the German amateur astronomer Johann Palitzsch finally spotted the returning comet. Edmund Halley thus is credited with proving that comets orbit the sun just as planets do. Edmund Halley (1656–1742) had died 16 years earlier, and the famous comet was named in his honor. Comets show the dependable clockwork operation of the solar system.

DECEMBER
26

1676. Dutch scientist Anton van Leeuwenhoek worked with early microscopes. His careful records show a major discovery today. Van Leeuwenhoek looked at water in which pepper had been steeped overnight. He saw living creatures which were many times smaller than ever seen before. Anton van Leeuwenhoek had discovered bacteria, and thus initiated the science of bacteriology. Microbes can cause disease but they also have many beneficial aspects. As examples, they enrich the soil, decompose waste, clean the water, help digest our food, and keep us healthy. These invisible, complex "factories" are an important gift from the Creator.

1831. A small ship called the HMS *Beagle* left England today, bound for the Pacific Ocean. On board was naturalist Charles Darwin. He later called this date "my real birthday." Over the next five years Darwin collected data and polished his evolutionary ideas. The ship returned to England five years later. Darwin waited until 1859 to publish his *Origin of Species* book.

DECEMBER 27

DECEMBER 28

1732. Benjamin Franklin's famous *Poor Richard's Almanac* was first advertised today. Franklin's purpose was to print "proverbial sentences, chiefly such as inculcated industry and frugality, as a means of procuring wealth, and thereby securing virtue." Typical entries: .

God helps them that help themselves.

Lost time is never found again.

The *Farmer's Almanac* still continues Ben Franklin's publication today. Unfortunately, the helpful proverbs have been largely replaced by astrology horoscopes and guesses at future weather.

1967. The name "black hole" was first used today by astronomer John Wheeler during a conference in New York City. This descriptive title is given  to certain massive stars which are thought to shrink drastically in size as they run low on nuclear fuel. The star it-self collapses to a mere point. The region around the star then experiences severe gravity from which not even light itself can escape. No black holes have yet been verified in space. There may be many black holes or perhaps none at all. If black holes do indeed exist, they are a testimony to the wearing down of the universe from its perfect created beginning, including the aging of stars.

1913. One of the most familiar dia-grams in astronomy first appeared to-day. At a science meeting in Atlanta, Ejnar Hertz and Henry Norris Russell showed a plot of star temperature ver-sus brightness. The graph gives an un-expected pattern. Numerous stars exist with particular temperature and brightness values. For other values of temperature and brightness, however, few or no stars exist. It thus appears that stars occur in par-ticular categories or kinds, somewhat similar to the cre-ated kinds of plants and animals. Stellar evolution is an attempt to explain how one kind of star slowly may change into another type. In truth, the stars, in all their variety, may well appear much as God made them on the fourth day of creation.

1952. Today Linus Pauling (1901–1994) published his discovery of the alpha-helix structure of proteins. This twist-ing pattern reveals the elegant artistry of the Creator in organizing complex chains of molecules. For his many dis-coveries, Pauling is the past century's best-known chemist. He also is the first person to receive Nobel prizes in two different fields — chemistry and peace.

• • • •

Imagine an evolutionary time scale with all of history tele-scoped into a single "cosmic year." According to this pro-posal, the alleged big bang occurred on January 1 and the earth formed much later, on September 25. In this view, mankind evolved only today, December 31, during the last moments of universe history. In contrast, the creation view places people at the completion of the creation week on day six. Biblically, mankind is not a mere afterthought of evolu-tionary time but instead is the centerpiece of creation.

REFERENCES

Asimov, Isaac. *Asimov's Chronology of Science and Discovery*. New York: Harper Collins, Inc., 1994.

Bobick, James, editor. Compiled by the Science and Technology Department of the Carnegie Library of Pittsburgh. *The Handy Science Answer Book*. Washington DC: Visible Ink Press, 1994.

Bunch, Bryan, and Alexander Hellenmans. *The Timetables of Technology*. New York: Simon and Schuster Inc., 1993.

Burnham, Robert. *Burnham's Celestial Handbook*. New York: Dover Publications, Inc., 1978.

Burnam, Tom. *The Dictionary of Misinformation*. New York: Harper and Row, 1986.

Collison, Robert. *Newnes Dictionary of Dates*. London: Newnes, 1966.

Douglas, George W. *The American Book of Days*. New York: H.W. Wilson Company, 1937.

Eley, Mary, editor. *Chase's Calendar of Events*. Chicago, IL: Contemporary Books, Inc., 1995.

Gillispie, Charles C., editor. *Dictionary of Scientific Biography*. Twenty volumes. New York: Charles Scribner's Sons, 1970.

Giscard, Valerie-Anne d'Esaing and Mark Young, editors. *Inventions and Discoveries*. New York: Facts on File, various years.

Gregory, Ruth W. *Special Days*. Secaucus, NJ: The Citadel Press, 1978.

Grun, Bernard. *The Timetables of History*. New York: Simon and Schuster, 1991.

Hatch, Jane M. *The American Book of Days*. New York: H.W. Wilson Co., 1978.

Hellemans, Alexander, and Bryan Bunch. *The Timetables of Science*. New York: Simon and Schuster, Inc., 1988.

Hoffman, Mark, editor. *The World Almanac and Book of Facts*. New York: World Almanac, annual.

Internet. Several information calendars are available at various locations. However, most of these calendars are notoriously unreliable. One accurate, comprehensive calendar is maintained by the Scope Systems Worldwide Industrial Electronics Repair and Services.

James, Peter, and Nick Thorpe. *Ancient Inventions*. New York: Ballantine Books, 1994.

Kane, Joseph Nathan. *Famous First Facts*. New York: H.W. Wilson Company, 1981.

Matthews, Peter, editor. *The Guinness Book of World Records*. New York: Facts on File, Inc., annual.

Millgate, Linda. *The Almanac of Dates*. New York: Harcourt Brace Javanovich, 1977.

Milner, Richard. *The Encyclopedia of Evolution*. New York: Facts on File, 1990.

Morris, Henry M. *History of Modern Creationism*. Green Forest, AR: Master Books, Inc., 1984.

Sims, Michael. *Darwin's Orchestra*. New York: Henry Holt and Company, 1997.

Spinard, Leaonard and Thelma Spinard. *Speaker's Lifetime Library*. West Nyack, NY: Parker Publishing Co., Inc., 1984.

Stewart, Robert. *The Illustrated Almanac of Historical Facts*. New York: Prentice Hall, 1992.

Williams, Neville. *Chronology of the Modern World*. New York: David McKay Company, Inc., 1966.

Wallechinsky, David. *History with the Boring Parts Left Out*. New York: Little, Brown and Company, 1995.

Name Index

Subject Index

SCRIPTURE INDEX

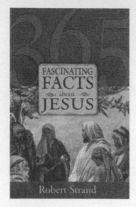

365 FASCINATING FACTS ABOUT JESUS
ROBERT STRAND

From over 100 sources, popular gift book author Robert Strand has compiled both common and little-known facts about Jesus Christ.

The Jesus that Strand uncovers is definitely the Christ of the Gospels, and the political, cultural, and religious times in which He lived are brought to life in this terrific book. Read about the traditions that Jesus grew up with, the historical facts about His birth, death, and resurrection, and man's ideas about Him vs. reality. Great as a reference book or gift, this collection of fascinating facts serves to illuminate "God With Us."

ISBN: 0-89221-488-0 • 216 pages • $10.99

365 FASCINATING FACTS ABOUT THE HOLY LAND
CLARENCE H. WAGNER, JR.

Written from the unique perspective of one American who has made Israel his home for 22 years, this remarkable compilation gives you a bird's-eye view of the Middle East, its people and customs. You will get glimpses into the lives of both Jews and Arabs, and marvel at the power of a region claiming Hebron, Bethlehem, Haifa, Tel Aviv, the Golan . . . and, of course, the City on a Hill, Jerusalem.

ISBN: 0-89221-489-9 • 216 pages • $10.99

Available at Christian bookstores nationwide.